J.M. Jordan
New York 7-74

T4-AEI-734

PHILOSOPHICAL CLASSICS
General Editor: PETER G. LUCAS

LEIBNIZ
DISCOURSE ON METAPHYSICS

LEIBNIZ

DISCOURSE ON
METAPHYSICS

A TRANSLATION FROM THE FRENCH
BASED ON THE DIPLOMATIC EDITION

by
PETER G. LUCAS
and
LESLIE GRINT

MANCHESTER UNIVERSITY PRESS

© 1953, P. G. LUCAS and LESLIE GRINT
Published by
The University of Manchester at
THE UNIVERSITY PRESS
316–324 Oxford Road
Manchester, 13

First published 1953
Reprinted, with minor corrections, 1961
Reprinted 1968

GB SBN 7190 0218 4

Printed in Great Britain by Butler & Tanner Ltd., Frome and London

It also emerges from this analysis that the controversy as to whether the principle of sufficient reason asserts merely that every event has a reason, or that every event has a good (morally good) reason has no meaning in relation to Leibniz the devout metaphysician, for whom rational order and moral goodness are completely synthesised; the controversy only has any meaning if Leibniz is transformed into a modern logician out of his time.

The Elements of the Metaphysics
God (§§ 1–7)

assumptions:
1. an absolutely perfect being
2. has perfect understanding (knowledge) and perfect will (acts, creates perfectly).

principles:
3. the absolute perfection of God's will or action and of his created works or the world is their 'dependence' on his understanding, in that (*a*) God never acts without a reason, and (*b*) all events in the world are in order.
4. there is a multiplicity of possible orders, among which God has willed the creation of the 'best' (simplest in decrees and richest in effects; affording the greatest felicity of spirits).
5. God's perfections are only partially knowable by men.

analogy:
the artificer and what he makes.

problems:
perfection; God's liberty; the universal order; laws of nature and miracles.

Substances (§§ 8–16)

assumptions:
1(*a*). all knowledge consists of propositions in subject-predicate form.

subordinate parts of his system in the form of other kinds of statements about God and substances, and in this way to effect his philosophical synthesis. For example his theory of knowledge is expressed in the form of an explanation of 'how God acts on the understanding of spirits', and the theory of conduct as an explanation of 'how God inclines our soul without necessitating it'; and similarly for dynamics and piety. But perhaps the most important opening offered by this kind of exposition is that it enables Leibniz to conceive and express the fundamental analogy of each substance ' expressing ' God and the universe, which we believe to have been the impulse that produced the act of philosophical synthesis in which Leibniz first conceived his system.

Some commentators make much of the 'occasional' character of all Leibniz's writing, a principle of interpretation which in this case would make the starting-point and manner of exposition merely a device deliberately adopted by Leibniz because he thought it would be acceptable to his audience, in particular Arnauld. There can be no doubt that this occasional or political character is an essential feature of Leibniz's thought, but it is a trivialisation merely to draw from it that Leibniz never really meant just what he said. Its place in the *Discourse* is a matter for investigation. In the opinion of the editor this manner of exposition is not deliberately and artfully adopted here by Leibniz but is the real order of the generation of his own thought and experience, and as such makes intelligible features of his mature philosophy that appear arbitrary if they are understood merely as developments out of his two great principles.

We offer here an analysis of the metaphysics as it is expounded in the first two sections of the *Discourse*, on God and substances. The principles of contradiction and sufficient reason will be seen to lie behind the principles listed under the heading of 'God' and again of 'substances', which correspond and to some extent repeat each other.

Malebranche), and the Spanish Jesuit metaphysics of Suarez and Molina.

The Metaphysics of the Discourse

The philosophy of Leibniz is known to all subsequent philosophy as founded on the two principles of contradiction and of sufficient reason, as he explicitly declared in the *Monadology* (§§ 31, 32 ' our reasoning is founded on two great principles . . .'). These principles can be shown to be the foundation, or part of the foundation, of the metaphysics of the *Discourse*, but they are not expounded as such for their own sake, as they are in the later writings. The mode of exposition of metaphysics in the *Discourse* gives a more genuine representation of Leibniz's thought than the later and better-known writings and for that reason will be briefly analysed here.

Within the sections on God and substances we can distinguish (in addition to the ' moral ' discourse) the following elements :—

What is propounded by him as his own new metaphysics, and, within this, (i) assumptions—what is taken for granted, either silently or by being asserted as generally accepted ; and (ii) ' principles '.

The re-interpretation or solution of metaphysical problems in terms of the new metaphysics, and within this, (i) development of the metaphysics in terms of analogies, and (ii) the application of the new metaphysics, with its analogical developments, to traditional and current problems of metaphysics.

The metaphysics is expounded first in the form of statements about a God with an understanding and a will, and again in the form of statements about substances and their attributes. That there is a God of this kind, and that all existents are substances having attributes is assumed, and the metaphysical principles are presented as consequences of the ' nature ' of God and of substances. This manner of exposition makes it easy for Leibniz to express the

INTRODUCTION   xix

of the metaphysics which he has already propounded. These leading concepts and principles (indicated in the following table) are thus the points of philosophical synthesis between metaphysics on the one hand, and action and knowledge of existence on the other.

The scheme which emerges is one of distinct universes of discourse, in which metaphysics is dominant and is connected to the other universes of discourse through the dependence of the general principles of each on metaphysical principles. This gives the following plan of the *Discourse*:—

1. Expression of the life of piety and primary metaphysical discourse relating to
    God

2. Primary metaphysical discourse, shown to be consonant with piety, relating to
    Substances

By this means metaphysical principles are established.

3. Dependent aspects of piety and dependent argument relating to : the metaphysics of natural philosophy
    (force and final causes), and the dependence on this of ' phenomena '

4. . . . the metaphysics of knowledge (ideas) and the dependence on this of what we know

5. . . . the metaphysics of ethics (grace and free will) and the dependence on this of conduct

6. . . . the metaphysics of piety and religion (spirits) and the dependence on this of the devout and religious life

(iv) *Contemporary Problems.*—Throughout the *Discourse* Leibniz inserts well-integrated statements of his attitude on traditional problems of metaphysics as such and of the metaphysics of natural philosophy, theory of knowledge, ethics and religion, and estimates of contemporary schools, in particular the materialists (following Gassendi and Hobbes), the Cartesians, and the occasionalists (following

rounded description and recommendation of the life of piety, and the following sections contain repeated allusions to the consonance of their detail with this life. We thus have the scheme:

1. Expression of the life of piety, relating to:		1. Primary metaphysical discourse relating to:
	1. God	
2. Dependent aspects of piety, relating to:		
	2. Substances	
		2. Dependent metaphysical argument relating to:
	3. Force and final causes	
	4. The human understanding	
	5. The human will	
	6. Piety and religion	

(iii) *Universes of Discourse (Epistemology)*.—The manner in which the last four topics can be dependent on the primary metaphysics is discussed by Leibniz in an article belonging to the section on substances (§ 10) and elsewhere in passing. This constitutes what would now be called the epistemological aspect of the system. The principles of the metaphysics of substances are required in 'philosophy and theology' but must not be used in the detail of natural philosophy, geometry, and moral philosophy (nor incidentally of politics and jurisprudence); metaphysics 'brings about no changes in phenomena'. Natural philosophy however has 'general principles' (comparable with presuppositions in later epistemology) which are metaphysical in character; and similarly with the understanding, the will and piety. In each of the four subjects Leibniz draws the leading concepts and principles at least partly from the subject itself, as it is known in ordinary practice; he then shows that though they are essential to correct knowledge of phenomena or correct action, they are not justifiable out of the subject itself, but can be developed and justified out

INTRODUCTION

'metaphysical' and 'moral' (sometimes 'practical') to distinguish the two modes, and commentators have used the terms 'metaphysical' and 'theological', the latter not entirely appropriately, in that it is not primarily a system of theological principles that is expressed and recommended in the passages characteristic of the second mode, but a devout and pious life. The moral philosopher, in this sense, does not need to trouble himself with the theological problem of reconciling freedom of the will and God's providence (§ 10). One of the grounds on which Leibniz recommends this life is that the kind of piety and devotion which the *Discourse* is intended to evoke causes problems in the dogmatic theology of the churches and the sects to disappear.

These two modes are continuously present throughout the work. Which, in the generation of Leibniz's philosophy, sprang originally from the other, is a matter for investigation. In the expression of his philosophy as we have it in the *Discourse* both are of fundamental and nearly equal importance, and if on the whole the metaphysics tends to be subordinate to the piety, this is a question of proportion which can only be assessed in the context of the rest of Leibniz's work, and taking into account that one of his concerns, which may have been before his mind when writing the *Discourse*, was the projected re-union of the churches under a universal rational metaphysical theology. Metaphysics and piety appear here in a philosophical synthesis mutually requiring and supporting each other.

If we consider the sequence of the exposition through the six topics enumerated above, we observe the following relations between the sections. Under the metaphysical aspect, only the first two sections (on God and substances) contain argument presented as original and self-contained; the rest of the *Discourse* is presented as dependent in different ways on what is regarded as having been established there. Under the aspect of piety the first section contains a

In addition to its independent value in itself, the *Discourse*, having a complete structure, may serve as a guide through Leibniz's subsequent writings each of which separately is only a partial expression of Leibniz's thought. For this purpose also it is important both to appreciate each of the elements separately and at the same time to grasp its position in the system.

This analysis is a series of reductions of the whole to its essential structure, each successive reduction being a more complex analysis underlying the previous more superficial analysis. It is followed by a detailed analysis of the primary metaphysics. The whole account is intended to be of service to the reader *after* he has read the *Discourse* and will scarcely be intelligible before.

(i) *Subject-Matter.*—The topics treated can be arranged in the following six sections:
1. God (§§ 1–7)
2. Substances (§§ 8–16)
3. Force and final causes (§§ 17–22)
4. The human understanding (§§ 23–29)
5. The human will (§§ 30–31)
6. Piety and religion (§§ 32–37)

Our division of the work into these sections is justified partly by the internal coherence of each, and partly by remarks at the beginning of the first article of each successive section, by means of which Leibniz indicates that he has concluded one subject and is passing to the next.

(ii) *Modes of Discourse* ('*metaphysical*' and '*moral*').—Throughout the work we can distinguish two modes of discourse which are in the closest association with each other. The one may be called logical, in that it proceeds by argument from premises to conclusions, the premises being presented as evident and the conclusions as intellectual insights validated primarily by the argument; the other is an expression of Leibniz's piety and an exhortation of the reader to a life of piety. Leibniz uses the terms

(The fact that Leibniz communicated with Arnauld immediately after writing the *Discourse* has sometimes been unjustifiably assumed to mean that he wrote it *for* Arnauld.) He sent to Arnauld in February 1686 not the *Discourse* itself but a list of the summaries as printed here in the table of contents—an astonishingly ill-judged act, for the headings are only imperfectly intelligible by themselves and Arnauld could not conceivably have gained from them a proper understanding of the system. He replied curtly, rejecting the doctrines, in particular those of §13, as alarming and offensive. Leibniz replied in a conciliatory tone and a correspondence ensued (Gerhardt, Ph. II) which lasted until March 1690. It brought some philosophical clarification, but contributed nothing to the main project of re-union.

Leibniz's first public attempt to introduce his system to natural philosophers was the publication in the *Journal des Savants* of June 1695 of an article with the title 'New System of the nature and of the communication of substances, and of the union between the soul and the body' ('*Système nouveau de la nature et de la communication des substances, aussi bien que de l'union qu'il y a entre l'âme et le corps*', Gerhardt, Ph. IV, 477). This article contains the substance of those parts of the *Discourse* which are indicated in its title. A controversy with Pierre Bayle ensued, in which Bayle's replies took the form of footnotes to the article 'Rorarius' in the first edition of his dictionary in 1697 and again at greater length in the second edition of 1702.

THE STRUCTURE OF THE DISCOURSE

The philosophical originality of the *Discourse of Metaphysics* consists primarily in its coherence as a system. Appreciation of this quality of the *Discourse* involves holding all its elements before the mental view simultaneously and in the complex order of interdependence in which Leibniz conceived them. This is not always easy, and the following analysis is intended to assist the reader.

An account of the particular doctrines of the *Discourse* as they are found in Leibniz's previous writings would involve a complete study of his early life. We confine ourselves here to propounding the following thesis, a form of which was published in *Der Begriff der Repräsentation bei Leibniz* by Paul Köhler (Berne, 1913).

There is no major element in the *Discourse* which cannot be found singly in earlier writings, except for the one idea of expression or representation—that each substance *expresses* God and the universe from a point of view. This is Leibniz's alternative picture to the picture which was then and still is common of a universe consisting of objects and animate beings which have their separate individual existences but act and are acted on in a mechanical or quasi-mechanical system. This new picture or metaphor of the universe as a system of representation provided the impulse which enabled Leibniz to synthesise his attitude to life, his religion and his various separate philosophical principles into the metaphysical system which is contained in the *Discourse*.[1]

The subsequent history of the doctrines of the *Discourse* would involve a complete study of Leibniz's very active life. He was not satisfied, as the modern scholar pretends to be, merely to put down the truth in writing; his first aim was to introduce the truth into the society in which he lived, in particular into the worlds of learning, of politics, and of religion. At moments which he believed to be propitious he tried out such parts of his system as seemed likely to be favourably received. We mention the two best-known incidents.

One of the political purposes for which Leibniz hoped to use the metaphysics of the *Discourse* was as the basis of a universal rational theology which would make possible the re-union of the churches. His first step was to test the impact of his system on Antoine Arnauld, the celebrated Jansenist.

---

[1] L. J. Russell holds that the impulse was provided not by the idea of representation, but by the idea that the predicate in every true affirmative proposition is contained in the subject (*Philosophy* XXX, 112, p. 84).

INTRODUCTION

Origin of the Discourse

The *Discourse* was written in the winter of 1685–6, when Leibniz was 39. Our evidence consists in a letter of 1/11 February 1686 from Leibniz to Landgraf Ernst von Hessen-Rheinfels enclosing a list of the headings to the articles for transmission to Arnauld (Gerhardt,[1] Ph. II, 11). In this letter he announces that 'lately' ('*dernière-ment*'), having had nothing to do for a few days, he has written 'a short discourse on Metaphysics' ('*un petit discours de Métaphysique*') which he has not yet been able to have copied. This *Discourse* is thus the earliest expression of Leibniz's philosophical thought in the form of a system —a name which it fully merits for its coherence, for the scope and originality of its philosophical synthesis, and for its concreteness as the expression of an attitude to life. It contains all the major elements of what he was later to call the system of the pre-established harmony, though not always fully explicitly and without using the terms 'monad' and 'pre-established'.

There is evidence that Leibniz subsequently regarded the time at which the *Discourse* was written as the time at which he first achieved a finally satisfactory philosophical system. He writes in 1695: 'I conceived this system some years ago . . .' (*New System . . .*, Gerhardt, Ph. IV, 477), and in reply to Foucher's objections to the *New System*, alludes to Horace's rule *nonumque prematur in annum*, i.e. in 1695 the system had been concealed for nine years (IV, 490). In May 1697, in a letter to Burnett, after describing his uncertainty and changes of opinion during his early years, he says he has been 'satisfied for 12 years' (III, 205).

[1] References in this Introduction are to *Die philosophischen Schriften von Gottfried Wilhelm Leibniz*, edited by C. J. Gerhardt.

is comprised in his notion, but solely why Judas the sinner is admitted to existence in preference to other possible persons. Of the original imperfection or limitation before sin, and of the degrees of grace . 48

XXXI. Of the motives of election, of faith foreseen, of *scientia media*, of the absolute decree, and that all reduces itself to the reason why God has chosen for, and resolved to admit to, existence such and such a possible person, the notion of whom contains such and such a sequence of graces and free actions, which puts an end to the difficulties at a single stroke . . 51

[PIETY AND RELIGION]

XXXII. Utility of these principles in the matter of piety and religion 54

XXXIII. Explanation of the commerce of the soul and the body, which has passed for inexplicable or for miraculous, and of the origin of confused perceptions 56

XXXIV. Of the difference of Spirits from other substances, souls or substantial forms, and that the immortality which is demanded involves memory . 57

XXXV. Excellence of Spirits, and that God considers them preferably to the other creatures. . 58

XXXVI. God is the monarch of the most perfect republic composed of all the Spirits, and the felicity of this city of God is his principal design. That Spirits express God rather than the world, but that the other substances express the world rather than God 60

XXXVII. Jesus Christ has disclosed to men the mystery and the admirable laws of the Kingdom of Heaven and the greatness of the supreme felicity which God prepares for those who love him. . 62

XXI. If mechanical rules depended on geometry alone without metaphysics, phenomena would be quite different 36

XXII. Reconciliation of the two ways, of which the one goes by final causes and the other by efficient causes, in order to satisfy both those who explain nature mechanically and those who have recourse to incorporeal natures 37

[The Human Understanding]

XXIII. To return to immaterial substances, it is explained how God acts on the understanding of spirits, and whether we always have the idea of what we think 40

XXIV. What is knowledge clear or obscure, distinct or confused, adequate or inadequate, intuitive or suppositive ; and definition nominal, real, causal, essential 41

XXV. In what case our knowledge is joined with contemplation of the idea 43

XXVI. That we have in us all ideas ; and of Plato's reminiscence 44

XXVII. How our soul can be compared to empty tablets, and how our notions come from the senses 45

XXVIII. God alone is the immediate object of our perceptions which exists outside us, and he alone is our light 46

XXIX. Yet we think immediately by our own ideas and not by those of God 48

[The Human Will]

XXX. How God inclines our soul without necessitating it ; that we have no right to complain, and we must not ask why Judas sins, since this free action

XIV. God produces different substances according to the different views which he has of the universe, and by the intervention of God the nature proper to each substance carries with it that what happens to one corresponds to what happens to all the others, without their acting immediately on one another . 22

XV. The action of one finite substance on another consists only in the increase in the degree of its expression conjoined with the diminution of that of the other, in as much as God has so formed them in advance that they accommodate themselves to one another 26

XVI. The extraordinary concourse of God is comprised in what our essence expresses, for this expression extends to everything, but it surpasses the forces of our nature or our distinct expression, which is finite and follows certain subordinate maxims . 27

[FORCE AND FINAL CAUSES]

XVII. Example of a subordinate maxim or law of nature. In which it is shown that God always conserves regularly the same force but not the same quantity of motion, against the Cartesians and several others 28

XVIII. The distinction between force and quantity of motion is important *inter alia* for judging that we must have recourse to metaphysical considerations separate from extension in order to explain the phenomena of bodies 31

XIX. Utility of final causes in Natural Philosophy 32

XX. Memorable passage of Socrates in the Phaedo of Plato against over-materialist philosophers . 34

1(*b*). all existence consists of multiplicity of substances and their attributes.
2. all substances act (change, have events in time).

principles:
3. every substance or subject (*a*) contains timelessly the reason for or ground of deducibility of the attribution to it of all its actual attributes (changes, events in time) or all its true predicates, and (*b*) is related to every other substance in one universal order.
4. these reasons and this order are one of many possible systems of reason and orders, and are the best ('principle of contingency or of the existence of things'); whereas the elements in God's understanding ('eternal truths') have one necessary order.
5. the grounds for the attribution of attributes to substances are only partly knowable by men.

analogy:
expression (each substance expresses, represents from one point of view, the universe).

problems:
identity of indiscernibles, constant number of substances, substantial forms, matter not merely extension, necessity and contingency, causation, miracles.

THE DYNAMICS OF THE DISCOURSE

The third main section of the *Discourse* (§§ 17-22)—that in which force is discussed—contains an argument with the Cartesians which may be found obscure and is expressed in words which had plainly not yet become a stable terminology. We reproduce here the outline of the argument in Leibniz's and in modern terms. The terms used by Leibniz which differ from modern terminology are enclosed in single quotation marks.

There is a law of conservation in dynamics to which Leibniz wishes to allude as an example of a metaphysically grounded law of nature, in order to support his argument that natural philosophy requires in scholastic terms, substantial forms, or in his own later term, monads. The doctrine of the Cartesians is that 'quantity of motion' is conserved, defined in Leibniz's terms as 'speed multiplied by size', or in modern terms as velocity multiplied by mass, namely momentum. 'Quantity of motion' is taken by the Cartesians to be equivalent to 'motive force', in modern terms energy; it is this equivalence that Leibniz wishes to refute.

Leibniz's thesis is that 'force' (energy) is conserved, and is not identical with 'quantity of motion' (momentum). He establishes this from the example of falling bodies. He assumes with the Cartesians that in the case of bodies being lifted, equal 'forces' will be required for equal products of 'weight' and 'height'; or in modern terms for equal work done. He transfers his concept of 'force' from lifting to falling by means of the assumption that a falling body theoretically acquires the 'force' to rise again to the height from which it fell—an assumption which is unsound in that it ignores the displacement of the earth due to the fall. He then draws on Galileo's principle that the 'speed acquired by a fall' is proportional to the square root of the 'height', to show that in the case of falling bodies, if 'force' is measured in what he maintains to be the correct way, by 'the quantity of the effect which it can produce' (work done), it is to be calculated as the square of the 'speed' multiplied by 'size', or mass multiplied by the square of the velocity, which is effectively equivalent to the modern formula kinetic energy equals $\frac{mv^2}{2}$. 'Force' is thus not identical with 'quantity of motion'; this is interpreted in § 18 as showing that 'force' requires metaphysical considerations, in that bodies, even for mechanics, must possess something other than their purely material attributes of 'size, figure and motion'. For modern mechanics what they possess is potential energy, which all bodies have by virtue of their position in space.

There is an allusion in § 21 to conservation of 'direction in sum', or in modern terms conservation of linear momentum. In a dynamical system all bodies in motion have a component of velocity in any given direction (the projection of their motion on this direction as an axis), and if the sum of the components for a closed system in motion, e.g. the universe as Leibniz conceives it, were not conserved, there would be stretching or contracting of the system in that direction.

BASIS OF THE TEXT

The Diplomatic Edition.—Students of Leibniz are indebted to the late Abbé Henri Lestienne for identifying Leibniz's autograph manuscript of the *Discourse on Metaphysics* and for an edition which reproduces the manuscript and its fair copy exactly, indicating by typographical devices the successive corrections and deletions. This was first published in 1907. We are informed in the edition of 1929 that the publication of an extensive commentary which was intended to accompany the text was delayed and finally prevented by the death of Lestienne on active service in 1915. The autograph MS. and the fair copy were in different sections of the Leibniz papers and had been listed separately by Bodemann under different titles in different sections of his Catalogue of the papers. Previous editions of the *Discourse* were taken from the fair copy only.

Lestienne's edition is now reprinted in the *Bibliothèque des Textes Philosophiques* (Vrin, Paris) and by kind permission of the publishers such parts of the material from it as may contribute in any way to philosophical understanding have been reproduced in this translation.

Lestienne claims to have followed the MS. exactly in all respects except for punctuation (regrettably) and for the subdivision of the articles into paragraphs. The original has no subdivisions. We have followed Lestienne's paragraphs.

The manuscripts reproduced by Lestienne are as follows:—

1. Autograph manuscript, entirely in Leibniz's hand, heavily corrected and revised (Bodemann, Theol. III, 1, *Traité sur les perfections de Dieu* . . .).

2. Copies A and C. A incomplete, C a fragment. Some corrections in Leibniz's hand, often faulty (Bodemann, ibid.).

3. Copy B, taken directly from the autograph MS. by a copyist and carefully corrected by Leibniz, with a few short additions (Bodemann, Phil. III, 7, *Discours de métaphysique* . . .). Contains a few copyist's errors not corrected by Leibniz and reproduced in the previous editions. Does not include the summaries of the articles.

We have also taken into account:

4. Copy of the list of summaries of the articles sent by Leibniz to Arnauld, printed from the original MS. by Grotefend and again from the MS. by Gerhardt (Ph. II, 12).

Lestienne distinguishes the following stages in the compilation of the text: (i) the original draft, (ii) marginal additions made to each page before writing the next, (iii) a further revision (the most important), (iv) insertion of the summaries at the head of each article, (v) three further revisions, (vi) insertions above the line in the original and in the additions, (vii) copy B, (viii) corrections and additions to B. He also gives the deletions in footnotes. To these we can add (ix) corrections and additions in the list of summaries sent to Arnauld.

To distinguish all these stages in the translation would greatly encumber the text with little profit to the reader, and as the successive revisions were all made within a very short time, to distinguish them chronologically can have no usable philosophical significance. We have therefore only distinguished between original draft and additions. The additions are shown between the signs * . . . †, and additions to additions thus ** . . . ††.

Many of the additions and deletions are the result of purely grammatical and stylistic alterations; these we have ignored. There are also a number of deleted matters of substance; these have been scrupulously retained, and shown in footnotes between square brackets. Successive deletions are given between the same brackets but separated by an oblique stroke. The test for retention was whether the deletion contained a word which had not been embodied in the final text of the same or adjacent sentences. The reader will appreciate that these deletions range from the correction of simple mistakes to the suppression of opinions on which Leibniz preferred not to commit himself, and will use due caution in attributing their substance to him.

The text of the translation is thus for the articles a reproduction of copy B corrected from the autograph MS. where B is faulty, with previous additions and deletions of substance shown, and with editor's punctuation and paragraphing; and for the summaries of the articles (which do not appear in B), a reproduction of them as in the list sent to Arnauld, also showing earlier additions and deletions.

List of Editions

1. *Briefwechsel zwischen Leibniz, Arnauld und dem Grafen Ernst von Hessen-Rheinfels*, herausgegeben von C. L. Grotefend. Hannover, 1846.
2. *Nouvelles lettres et opuscules inédits de Leibniz*, par A. Foucher de Careil. Paris, 1857.
3. *Die philosophischen Schriften von Gottfried Wilhelm Leibniz*, herausgegeben von C. J. Gerhardt. Berlin, 1880, Vol. IV.
4. *Leibniz. Discours de métaphysique*. Edition collationnée avec le texte autographe présentée et annotée par Henri Lestienne. Paris, 1907. Reprinted Vrin, Paris, 1929 and subsequently. (The definitive text.)
5. Several subsequent popular editions, separately and in selected works, including: (*a*) edited H. Schmalenbach, Leipzig, 1914, (*b*) edited Thouverez, Paris, (*c*) edited L. Prenant, Paris.

INTRODUCTION

Translation into English

Leibniz. *Discourse on Metaphysics, Correspondence with Arnauld and Monadology.* Translated by George R. Montgomery. La Salle, Ill. 1902. Second edition revised by Albert R. Chandler.

PRINCIPLES OF TRANSLATION

Authenticity—the strictest achievable truth to the original (not adaptation to the supposed needs and limitations of a twentieth-century reader)—is the ideal by which this translation would be judged. We have aimed at internal consistency and agreement with the English usage of Leibniz's contemporaries (without gratuitous archaisms), in particular with the usage of the edition of the Leibniz-Clarke correspondence published in 1717 with French and English on facing pages. Leibniz's command of the French language was not perfect, and at a number of points the translation is a rendering of the German or the Latin which can be plainly seen behind some of the stranger sentences. It is hoped that the somewhat gauche manner of the original has been reproduced. A principle of particular importance in a philosophy so strongly tied to its analogies as Leibniz's is that no alien metaphors, images and as far as possible no conspicuously alien etymological roots should be introduced. The practice of incorporating comment and interpretation into the text in the form of expansion or paraphrase is objectionable; here they have been strictly segregated into footnotes.

The word 'esprit', for which spirit, soul, mind, head, heart, and person might all have been used by an English writer, has been translated throughout as 'spirit' in order to avoid introducing arbitrary distinctions.

INTRODUCTION xxix

Authorities.—In addition to the usual works of reference the following have been consulted :—

GASTON CAYROU : *Le français classique. Lexique de la langue du XVIIe siècle* . . . 6th edition, 1948.

RANDLE COTGRAVE : *A French and English dictionary.* Various editions, 1611–73.

GUY MIEGE : *A new dictionary French and English 1677, 1679, 1691.*

INDEX OF PERSONS

Alexander	13	Hobbes	42 n. ; xix
Aristotle	31, 45, 47	Judas	48, 50
Arnauld	xiii–xv, xxi	Julius Caesar	20, 21
Augustin, St.	51	Malebranche	12 n., 48 n. ; xx
Averroes	47	Molina	51 n. ; xx
Bayle	xv	Paul, St.	50 n., 53–4
Calderon	19 n.	Peter, St.	20 n., 21 n.
Copernicus	45	Plato	18 n., 34–6, 44–5
Descartes	5 n., 12 n., 28–31, 40 ; xix, xxiii–iv	Snell van Royen	39–40
		Socrates	34–6
Fermat	39	Spinoza	5 n.
Galileo	30	Suarez	51 n. ; xx
Gassendi	xix	Teresa, St.	55 n.
Heliodorus of Larissa	39	Thomas, St.	14, 17
Hessen-Rheinfels, Graf Ernst v.	xiii	William of St. Amour	47

DISCOURSE
ON
METAPHYSICS

Words shown between the signs * . . . † are additions to the first draft, and between the signs ** . . . †† additions to additions. Words deleted by Leibniz from the first draft are shown in footnotes between square brackets. See p. xxvi. All matter in the footnotes which is not Leibniz's own words or translation of them is printed in italics.

DISCOURSE ON METAPHYSICS[1]

I. Of the divine perfection and that God does everything in the manner most to be desired.

[a]*The notion of God which is the most widely received and the most significant that we have is well enough expressed in these terms, that† God is an absolutely perfect being, *but the consequences of this do not receive enough consideration; and to go into them further, it is apposite to remark that there are in nature several **quite different†† perfections, that God possesses them all together, and that each belongs to him to the most sovereign degree.

[b]We also need to know what perfection is, and this is a sure enough mark of it, namely that† the forms or natures which are not susceptible of an ultimate degree are not perfections, as for example *the nature of† number or of figure. For the greatest number of all (or the number of all numbers) as well as the greatest of all figures imply contradiction, but the greatest knowledge and omnipotence

---

[a] *This sentence was repeatedly corrected by Leibniz. He first wrote:* [a']God is an absolutely perfect being, [such that he possesses all the perfections together and to the most sovereign degree,[a"] and here it is well to remark that all] the forms or natures which are not susceptible of an ultimate degree [are not of the number of the perfections, as for example] number . . .

[a'] *addition:* [The most ancient and the most widely received idea that we can form of God is that] . . .

[a"] *addition:* [that is what everybody remains agreed on, though it seems that] the consequences . . .

[b] [In order the better to understand/know] what perfection is

---

[1] *The manuscript and copy have no title. The work has become known under this name from Leibniz's allusion to it in his letter to Graf Ernst von Hessen-Rheinfels of 1/11 February 1686 as "un petit discours de métaphysique" (Introduction, p. xiii).*

4   DISCOURSE ON METAPHYSICS

*a**contain no impossibility†. Consequently *power and knowledge† are perfections, and *b**in as much as they† belong to God, *they have no limits†.

Whence it follows that God possessing supreme and infinite wisdom acts in the most perfect manner, not only in the metaphysical sense but also morally speaking; which can be expressed with regard to ourselves thus, that the more we are enlightened and informed about the works of God, the more we shall be disposed to find them excellent and entirely satisfying to every desire that we could have had.

*II. Against those who maintain that *c*there is no goodness in the works of God, or that the rules of goodness and beauty are arbitrary.*

Thus I am far removed from the sentiment of those who maintain that there are no rules of goodness and of perfection in the nature of things, or in the ideas that God has of them, and that the works of God are good only because *of the formal reason that† God made them. For if that were so, God knowing that he is the author of them had no need to look upon them afterwards and find them good, as is testified by Holy Scripture, which only seems to have made use of this anthropology [1] in order to teach us *d*that their excellence makes itself known when they are looked at in themselves, even when we do not reflect on this purely extrinsic denomination which refers the works to their cause. *Which is the more true, in that it is by consideration of the works that one can discover the work-

a [imply none,]
b belong to God [in the most unlimited manner.]
c [the beauty and goodness of things only depend on the opinion of men]
d [that there is goodness in them]

---

[1] *in the obsolete sense of* " *a way of speaking of God, after the manner of men, by attributing human parts and passions to him* " (*O.E.D.*).

man. Hence these works must bear his character in them.† I confess that the contrary sentiment appears to me extremely dangerous and to verge closely on that of *ᵃ*the most recent innovators†, whose opinion is that the beauty of the universe and the goodness which we attribute to the works of God are only chimeras of men who conceive God after their own manner. Also, by saying that things are not good by any rule of goodness but by God's will alone, it seems to me that one unthinkingly destroys all love of God and all his glory. For why praise him for what he has done, if he would be equally praiseworthy in doing just the contrary? Where then will be his justice and his wisdom, if there only remains a certain despotic power, if will takes the place of reason, and if, according to the definition of tyrants, what pleases the most powerful is just by that alone? Besides which, it seems that every will supposes some reason for willing, and that this reason is naturally anterior to the will. That is why I also find altogether strange the expression of *ᵇ*certain other philosophers† who say that the eternal truths of metaphysics and of geometry *and consequently also the rules of goodness, **of justice†† and of perfection,† are only effects of God's will, whereas it seems to me that they are only consequences of his understanding, which assuredly no more depends on his will than does his essence.

III. Against those who believe that God could have done better.

Neither am I able to approve the opinion of some ᶜmoderns who boldly maintain that what God does is not of the highest degree of perfection, and that he could have acted much better. For it seems to me that the consequences of this sentiment are altogether contrary to the glory of God. *Uti minus malum habet rationem boni, ita minus*

ᵃ [the Spinozists, who conceive that the beauty and harmony]
ᵇ [Monsieur Descartes]
ᶜ [modern scholastics]

bonum habet rationem mali.[1] And to act with less perfection than one could have acted, is to act imperfectly. To point out that an architect could have done better[a] is to find fault with his work. This also goes against Holy Scripture, when it assures us of the goodness of the works of God. For since imperfections descend to infinity, in whatever way God had made his works they would still have been good in comparison with less perfect works, *if that were enough :† but a thing is barely praiseworthy if it is only to be praised in this way. I believe also that an infinity of passages will be found in Divine Scripture and the Holy Fathers in favour of my sentiment, but that hardly any will be found for that of these [b]moderns, *which in my opinion is unknown to all antiquity, and is only based on our having too little knowledge of the general harmony of the universe and of the hidden reasons for the conduct of God which makes us judge rashly that many things could have been improved. Besides which these moderns take their stand† on some unsolid subtleties, for they imagine that nothing is so perfect that there is not something more perfect, which is an error.[c]

They also believe that they are providing thus for the liberty of God, as if it were not the highest liberty to act perfectly, according to sovereign reason. For to believe that God acts in anything without having any reason for his will, *besides that it seems that this cannot be†, is a sentiment which conforms little with his glory ; for example let us suppose that God chooses between A and B,

[a] [for the same cost]
[b] [new scholastics who rely only] on some unsolid . . .
[c] [for example, there is an infinity of regular figures, but one is the most perfect, namely the circle ; if a triangle had to be made and there was no determination of the sort of triangle, God would assuredly make an equilateral triangle, because absolutely speaking, this is the most perfect.]

---

[1] "As the less evil contains an element of good, so the less good contains an element of evil."

and that he takes A without having any reason for preferring it to B, I say that this action of God would at least not be praiseworthy; for all praise ought to be founded in some reason, which is lacking here *ex hypothesi*. Whereas I hold that God does nothing for which he does not deserve to be glorified.

IV. That love of God demands entire satisfaction and acquiescence concerning what he does, ^awithout our having therefor to be quietists.

General knowledge of this great truth that God always acts in the most perfect and most desirable manner possible is, in my opinion, the foundation of the love *that we owe to† God above all, ^bsince he who loves *seeks his satisfaction in† the felicity or perfection of the object loved ^c*and of his actions. *Idem velle et idem nolle vera amicitia est.*[1]† And I believe that it is difficult to love God well if one is not disposed to will what he wills, even if one had the power to change his will. Indeed those who are not satisfied with what God does appear to me to resemble disaffected subjects^d whose intention is not very different from that of rebels.

I hold then that according to these principles for acting conformably to the love of God it is not enough to have patience perforce, but we must be truly satisfied with all that has happened to us according to his will. I mean this acquiescence as to the past. For as to the future, we do not have to be quietists and wait ridiculously with

^a *Arnauld correspondence*: " without . . . quietists " *omitted.*
^b [and of a true contentment for those who love him, since loving is nothing other than finding pleasure]
^c [and consequently this sovereign goodness, this immutable justice, this profound wisdom, this power without limits]
^d [of a king or of a republic]

---

[1] " To will the same and not to will the same is true friendship."

folded arms for what God will do, according to the sophism that the ancients used to call λόγον ἄεργον, lazy reason, but we must act according to the presumptive will of God, as far as we can judge of it, *trying with all our power to contribute to the general good, and particularly to the adornment and perfection of that which touches us, or of that which is near to us, and so to speak within reach.† For if the event may perhaps show that God did not in this instance wish our good will to have its effect, it does not follow from this that he did not wish us to do what we did. On the contrary, *as he is the best of all masters, all that he ever asks is a right intention, and† it is for him to know the proper time and place for letting good designs prosper.

V. In what the rules of perfection of the divine conduct consist, and that the simplicity of the ways is in balance with the richness of the effects.

It is enough then to have confidence in God that he does everything for the best, and that nothing can harm those who love him ; but to know the particular reasons which moved him to choose this order of the universe, to suffer sins, to dispense his saving graces in a certain way, exceeds the forces of a finite spirit, especially when it has not yet attained enjoyment of the vision of God.

Yet some general remarks can be made touching the conduct of providence in the government of things. One can say then that[a] he who acts perfectly is like an excellent geometer who knows how to find the best constructions for a problem ; *or like a good architect who utilises his site and the funds destined for the building in the most advantageous manner, leaving nothing which offends or which falls short of the beauty of which it is susceptible ; like a good paterfamilias who puts his capital to use in such a way that nothing is left waste or barren ;† like a

[a] [that which encloses more reality in less volume is more perfect]

skilful engineer who makes his effect by choosing the least difficult way; like a talented author who encloses a maximum of realities in the least possible volume. Now the most perfect of all beings and those which occupy the least volume, that is to say which hinder each other least, are spirits, and their perfections are the virtues. That is why we must not doubt that [a]the felicity of spirits is the principal aim of God, and that he carries it out as far as the general harmony permits. *Of this we shall say more later.

As concerns the simplicity of God's ways, this holds properly with regard to means, as on the contrary the variety, richness and abundance in them hold with regard to ends or effects. And the one must be in balance with the other, as the costs destined for a building with the size and beauty that is expected of it. It is true that nothing costs God anything, **less indeed than it costs a philosopher to make hypotheses for the fabrication of his imaginary world, since God has only to make decrees in order to let a real world be born;†† but, in the matter of wisdom, decrees or hypotheses represent expenses in proportion as they are more independent of one another: for reason desires that multiplicity of hypotheses or principles should be avoided, in **almost†† the same way as the simplest system is always preferred in astronomy.†

VI. God does nothing out of order, and it is impossible even to feign events which are not regular.

God's wills or actions are commonly divided into ordinary and extraordinary. But it is well to consider that God does nothing out of order. Thus what passes for extraordinary is so only with regard to some particular order established among creatures. For as regards the universal order, everything conforms to it. This is so true that not only does nothing happen in the world which is

[a] [the greatest perfection of spirits is the aim of God as of nature]

absolutely irregular, but one cannot even feign such a thing. For let us suppose, for example, that someone makes a number of marks on paper quite at random, as do those who practise the ridiculous art of geomancy. I say that it is possible to find a geometrical line, the notion of which is constant and uniform according to a certain rule, such that this line passes through all these points, and in the same order as the hand had marked them.

And if someone drew in one stroke a line which was now straight, now circular, now of another nature, it is possible to find a notion or rule, or equation common to all the points on this line, in virtue of which these same changes must occur. *And there is no face, for example, the outline of which **does not form part of a geometrical line and†† cannot be traced in one stroke by a certain movement according to rule.† But when a rule is very complex what conforms to it passes for irregular.

Thus one can say that in whatever way God had created the world, it would always have been regular and in a certain general order. But God has chosen the one which is the most perfect, that is to say the one which is at the same time the simplest *in hypotheses† and the richest *in phenomena†, as a geometrical line might be, of which the construction was easy and the properties and effects were very admirable and of great extent. *I make use of these comparisons[a] in order to sketch some imperfect resemblance of the divine wisdom, and in order to say something which may at least elevate our spirit to conceive in some sort that which cannot be adequately expressed. But I do not claim to explain thereby this great mystery on which the whole universe depends.†

[a] [however remote they may be]

VII. That miracles are in conformity with the general order, although they are counter to subordinate maxims. Of what God desires or permits, ᵃand of general or particular will.

Now since nothing can be done which is not in order, one can say that miracles are as much in order as natural operations, so-called because they are in conformity with certain subordinate maxims which we call the nature of things. For one can say that this nature is only a habit of God, from which he can dispense himself because of a reason stronger than that which moved him to make use of these maxims.

As regards general or particular wills, according to how one takes the matter, one can say that God does everything according to his *most† general will, which is in conformity with the most perfect order which he has chosen; but one can also say that he has particular wills which are exceptions to the said subordinate maxims, for the most general of the laws of God which rules the whole sequence of the universe has no exceptions.

*One can also say that God wills everything that is an object of his particular will; but as regards the objects of his general will, such as are the actions of other [1] creatures, in particular of those which are reasonable, in which God wishes to concur, one must distinguish: for if the action is good[ᵇ] in itself, one can say that God wills it **and sometimes commands it even when it does not happen††; but if it is bad in itself and only becomes good by accident, because the sequence of things, ** and in particular punishment and satisfaction,[2]†† corrects its malignity and recompenses the evil with interest, with the result that in the end there is more perfection in the whole sequence than if all the evil had not happened, it must be said that

ᵃ [by a] general . . .   ᵇ [or indifferent]

---

[1] " other creatures " *strictly makes nonsense; the sense intended is presumably* " other actions than his own, namely those of creatures ".

[2] *in the sense of* " reparation ".

God permits it and not that he wills it, although he concurs in it because of the laws of nature which he has established and because he knows how to draw from it a greater good.†

VIII. In order to distinguish the actions of God and of creatures we explain in what the notion of an individual substance consists.

It is difficult enough to distinguish the actions of God from those of creatures[a]; for there are some [1] who believe that God does everything, and others [2] imagine that all he does is to conserve the force which he has given to creatures: *the sequel will show how far the one or the other can be said.† Now since actions and passions properly belong to individual substances (*actiones sunt suppositorum* [3]), it will be necessary to explain what such a substance is.

It is indeed true that when several predicates are attributed to the same subject and this subject is not attributed to any other, it is called an individual substance; but that is not enough, and such an explanation is only nominal. We must therefore consider what it is to be truly attributed to a certain subject.

Now it is a fact that all *true† predication has some foundation in the nature of things, and when a proposition is not identical, that is to say when the predicate is not expressly comprised in the subject, it must be comprised in it virtually, and that is what the Philosophers call *in-esse* *when they say that the predicate is in the subject.† Thus the term of the subject must always in-

[a] [and also the actions and passions of these same creatures]

---

[1] *the occasionalists, following Malebranche ("De la recherche de la vérité", 1674f).*
[2] *the Cartesians.*
[3] *" actions belong to supposita "—suppositum is a term in scholastic metaphysics for the being that is the subject of predicates or accidents.*

clude that of the predicate, so that whoever understood perfectly the notion of the subject would also judge that the predicate belongs to it.

This being so, we can say that the nature of an individual substance or of a complete being is to have a notion so complete that it is sufficient[a] to comprise and to allow the deduction from it of all the predicates of the subject to which this notion [b]is attributed. Whereas an accident is a being the notion of which does not include all that can be attributed to the subject to which this notion is attributed. [c]Thus *the quality of King which belongs to Alexander the Great,† *in abstraction from the subject, is not sufficiently determined for an individual, and† does not include *the other qualities of the same subject, nor† all that the notion of this Prince comprises; whereas God seeing the individual notion *or hæcceity [1]† *of Alexander† sees in it at the same time the foundation and reason of all the predicates that can be truly said of him, as for example that he would conquer Darius and Porus, *even to the point of knowing from it *a priori* (and not by experience)† whether he died a natural death or by poison, *which we can only know by history†. *Also, when we consider well the connection of things, we can say that there are at all times in [d]the soul of Alexander vestiges of all that has happened to him and the marks of all that will happen to him, and even traces of all that happens in the universe, although it belongs only to God to recognise them all.[e]†

[a] [in itself] [b] [belongs]
[c] Thus [the circular figure of the ring of Gyges/Polycrates] does not include all that the notion of this [individual ring] comprises; whereas God, seeing the individual notion of [this ring, as that it will be swallowed by a fish and nevertheless returned to its master]
[d] [this ring]
[e] [I speak here as if it were assured that this ring had a consciousness/is a substance.] (*Cf.* § *11*)

---

[1] " thisness ".

IX. *That each single substance expresses the whole universe after its own manner, and that in its notion all its events are comprised with all their circumstances and all the sequence of external things.*

There follow from this several notable paradoxes, as among others that it is not *ᵃ*true that two substances should resemble each other entirely and differ *solo numero*, *ᵇ**and that what St. Thomas assures us on this point of angels or intelligences (*quod ibi omne individuum sit species infima*) [1] is true of all substances, **provided one takes the specific differentia, as do geometers with regard to their figures†† ;† and that a subject can only *begin by creation and† perish by annihilation ; that one cannot divide a substance into two nor make one out of two, and thus that the number of substances does not augment or diminish naturally although they are often transformed.

Furthermore every substance *is like a **whole†† world and like a mirror **of God or†† of all the universe, which each expresses after its own fashion, much as the same town is variously represented according to the different situations of the man who is looking at it. Thus the universe is in some sort multiplied as many times as there are substances, and the glory of God is also redoubled by the same number of wholly different representations of his work. One can even say that every substance† bears in some sort the character of God's infinite wisdom and omnipotence, and imitates him as far as it is capable. For it expresses, albeit confusedly, all that happens in the universe, past, present or future, and this has some resem-

ᵃ [possible]
ᵇ [and that if bodies are substances, it is not possible that their nature should consist solely in size, figure and movement, but that something else is needed] (*Cf.* § *11*)

---

[1] " that with them every individual is a lowest species "—*i.e. every individual constitutes a species, the lowest species (next above individual) each having only one member.*

blance to an infinite perception or knowledge; and as all other substances express this one in their turn *and accommodate themselves to it†, one can say that it extends its power over all the others in imitation of the omnipotence of the Creator.

X. *That the opinion that there are substantial forms has something sound to it, but that these forms bring about no changes in phenomena and must not be used to explain particular effects.*

It seems that the ancients[a] as well as so many able men accustomed to profound meditation who taught theology and philosophy a few centuries ago, and of whom some are estimable for their holiness, had some knowledge of what we have just said, and that is what made them introduce and maintain substantial forms which today are so decried. But these men are not so far from the truth or so ridiculous as the common run of our new philosophers imagines.

I agree that consideration of these forms is of no service in *the detail of† natural philosophy,[1] and must not be used for explaining phenomena in particular. And it was in this that our scholastics failed, and the Physicians [2] of past times following their example, believing that they could account for the [b]properties of bodies by mentioning forms and qualities without going to the pains of examining the manner of operation; as if one were willing to content oneself with saying that a clock has the horodictic quality resulting from its form, without considering in what all this consists. *This may [c]indeed suffice for the

[a] [in distinguishing ens per se from ens per accidens [3] and introducing substantial forms]
[b] [phenomena]   [c] [perhaps]

---

[1] *here and at all subsequent occurrences:* "physique".
[2] "Médecins".   [3] "being in itself"—"being as accident".

man who buys it,† *provided that he leaves the care of it to someone else.†

But this failure and misuse of forms must not make us reject something, knowledge of which is so necessary in Metaphysics, that without it I hold that we are quite unable to know *a* the first principles or to elevate the spirit enough to know incorporeal natures and the marvels of God.

Yet as a Geometer has no need to trouble his spirit with the famous labyrinth of the composition of the continuum,[1] *and no moral philosopher, and still less a jurisconsult or politician, needs to trouble himself with the great difficulties that concern the reconciliation of free will with the providence of God,† since the Geometer can complete all his demonstrations, *and the politician bring to an end all his deliberations† without entering into these discussions, though they are necessary and important in philosophy *and theology :† likewise a Natural Philosopher[2] can account for his experiments using now *simpler† experiments already made, now geometrical and mechanical demonstrations, without needing*b* general considerations which belong to another sphere; and if he uses the*c* concourse of God, or of some soul, Arche[3] or other thing of this nature, he is extravagating as much as a man who in an important practical deliberation would enter into high reasoning about the nature of destiny or of our liberty; as indeed men make this mistake often enough unthinkingly, when they trouble their spirit with the consideration of fate and even are sometimes turned aside thereby from some good resolution or some necessary provision.

a [the principles of things]
b [considerations of substantial forms]   *c* [extraordinary]

---

[1] *i.e. the puzzle as to whether for instance a line is continuous or is composed of minute discrete parts.*
[2] " Physicien ".   [3] " first principle ".

DISCOURSE ON METAPHYSICS

*XI. That the meditations of the Theologians and philosophers who are called scholastics are not to be despised *entirely†.*

I know that I am advancing a great paradox in claiming to rehabilitate in some sort the ancient philosophy and to recall *postliminio* [1] the almost banished substantial forms[a]; but perhaps I shall not be lightly condemned when it is known that I have long meditated on modern philosophy, that I have given much time to the experiments of natural philosophy and the demonstrations of Geometry, and that I was for a long time persuaded of the vanity of these Beings, which in the end I was obliged to re-admit in spite of myself and as it were perforce, after researches of my own which made me recognise that our moderns do less than justice to St. Thomas and to other great men of that time and that the sentiments of scholastic philosophers and theologians are much sounder than is imagined, provided that they are used appositely and in their place. I am even persuaded that if some exact and meditative spirit would take the trouble to elucidate and digest their thoughts, in the manner of analytic Geometers, he would find in them a treasury of many very important and wholly demonstrative truths.

XII. [b]That the notions which consist in extension contain something imaginary and cannot constitute the substance of [c]body.

But to take up again the thread of our considerations, I believe that anyone who meditates on the nature of

[a] [although I only do this *ex hypothesi* in so far as one can say that bodies are substances] *(deleted only in the copy B; similar deletions in § 12(a), § 34(a) and § 35(a); cf. also § 8(e), § 9(b) and p. vi)*

[b] [The qualities of bodies] which consist . . .

[c] [bodies]

---

[1] " across the threshold " ; *a term used of the resumption of citizen rights after they had been lost or in abeyance.*

substance, which I have explained above, will find[a] that the whole nature of body does not consist solely in extension, that is to say in size, figure and motion, but that there must necessarily be *recognised in it† something which is related to souls and which is commonly called substantial form, though it brings about no changes in phenomena, no more than does the soul of beasts, if they have one. It can even be demonstrated[b] that the notion of size, figure and motion is not so distinct as is imagined, and that it includes something imaginary and relative to our perceptions, as are *also (although much more so)† colour, heat and other similar qualities, of which it can be doubted whether they are truly present in the nature of things outside us. That is why these kinds of qualities cannot constitute any substance. And if there were no other principle of identity in bodies than what we have just said, a body would never subsist for more than a moment.

*Yet the souls and substantial forms of other bodies are very different from intelligent souls, which alone know their actions, and which not only do not perish naturally, but also retain for ever **the foundation of†† their knowledge of what they are ; which makes them alone susceptible of punishment and reward and makes them citizens of the republic of the universe, of which God is the monarch ; whence it follows that all other creatures must serve them, of which we shall speak at greater length presently.†

XIII. *As the individual notion of each person contains once and for all everything that will ever happen to him, there are to be seen in this the proofs* a priori *or reasons† of the truth of every event, or why the one has happened rather than another ; but*

[a] [that bodies are not substances in strict metaphysics (which was indeed the sentiment of the Platonics)] and that the whole nature . . . (*deleted only in B ; cf.* § *11*)

[b] [that extension is not a notion clearly and distinctly known]

these truths, although assured, are none the less contingent, being founded on the free will of God or of creatures.[a] *It is true that their choice always has its reasons, but they incline without necessitating.*[1]

But before proceeding further we must try to meet a great difficulty which may arise from the foundations which we have laid above. We have said that the notion of an individual substance contains once and for all everything that can ever happen to it, and that on considering this notion all that could be truly propounded of it is to be seen in it, as we can see in the nature of the circle all the properties that can be deduced from it. But it seems that this will destroy the difference between contingent and necessary truths, [b]that human liberty will have no more place,[2] and that an absolute fate will reign over all our actions as well as over all the other events in the world. To which I reply that we must distinguish between what is certain and what is necessary: everybody agrees that future contingents are assured, since God foresees them; but for all that, it is not admitted that they are necessary. But (it will be said) if a conclusion can be deduced infallibly from a definition or notion, it will be necessary. Now we are maintaining that all that is to happen to any person is already comprised virtually in his nature or notion, as are the properties in the definition of the circle, *thus the difficulty still subsists.† To meet it soundly, I say that connection or consecution is of two sorts: the one is absolutely necessary, of which the contrary implies

[a] [although grounds are to be seen in it for judging which is the more reasonable and consequently assured,] the choice of which . . .
[b] [that all the fate of the Stoics will take the place of liberty]

[1] " incline without necessitating " *is a common phrase in the literature of fortune, destiny and free-will. The stars may incline, but without necessitating, that is, man may escape his destiny, as for instance in Calderon's play* " Life is a dream ". *The sense here is of course quite different.*
[2] " n'aura plus aucun lieu ".

contradiction, and this deduction has its place among [1] the eternal truths, such as are those of geometry; the other is only necessary *ex hypothesi*, and so to speak by accident, but in itself is contingent, the contrary implying no contradiction. And this connection is founded not merely on pure ideas and on God's understanding alone, but also on his free decrees *and on the sequence of the universe.

Let us take an example: [a]since Julius Caesar will become perpetual dictator and master of the republic and will overthrow the liberty of the Romans,† this action is comprised in his notion, for we suppose that it is the nature of such a perfect notion of a subject to comprise everything, in order that the predicate may be included in it, *ut possit inesse subjecto* [2]. It might be said that it is not by virtue of this notion or idea[b] that he must commit this action, since it is only appropriate to him because God knows all. But it is to be insisted that his nature or form corresponds to this notion, and since God has imposed on him this person, it is henceforth necessary for him to satisfy it. *I could reply with the example of future contingents, for they do not yet have anything real except in the[c] **understanding and will†† of God, and since God has there given them this form in advance, they will have to correspond to it none the less.

But I prefer to meet difficulties rather than to excuse them by the example of some other similar difficulties, and what I am going to say will serve to throw light on the one as well as the other.† It is here then that we must apply the distinction between connections, and I say that what happens in conformity with its antecedents is assured, but that it is not necessary, and if anyone did the contrary,

[a] [since St. Peter will deny our Lord,] this action ...
[b] [or nature] [c] [idea]

---

[1] "a lieu dans"; *but cf.* note [2], p. 19.
[2] "in order that it may be in the subject".

DISCOURSE ON METAPHYSICS 21

he would not do anything impossible *in itself, although it is impossible (*ex hypothesi*) that this should happen.† For if any man were capable of completing the whole demonstration, by virtue of which he could prove this connection of *a**the subject who is Caesar and the predicate which is his successful enterprise,† he would in fact reveal that *b* *the future dictatorship of Caesar† has its ground in his notion or nature, *that one can see in it a reason why he resolved rather to cross the Rubicon than to stop at it and why he won rather than lost the day at Pharsalus,† and that it was reasonable and consequently assured that this would happen, but not that it is necessary in itself nor that the contrary implies contradiction. *In **almost†† the same way as it is reasonable ** and assured†† that God will always do the best, although that which is less perfect implies no contradiction.*c*†

*d*For it would be found that this demonstration *of this predicate of Caesar† *is not as absolute as those of numbers or of geometry, but that it† supposes the sequence of things that God has freely chosen and which is founded on the first free decree of God, the import of which is always to do what is most perfect, and on the decree which God made (following the first) with regard to human nature, which is that man will always do *(although freely)† that which appears to him best. Now every truth which is founded on these sorts of decrees is contingent, although it is certain ; for these decrees do not change the possibility of things, and, as I have already said, although God always chooses the best assuredly, that does not prevent that which is less perfect from being *and remaining† possible in itself, even though it will not happen, for it is not its impossibility but its imperfection which makes God

---

a [the subject who is St. Peter and the predicate which is his denial] he would reveal that [this fact] has . . .

b [the obligation]   *c* [in itself]

d [This demonstration supposes the axiom that] the sequence of things . . .

reject it. Now nothing is necessary of which the opposite is possible.

*We shall be in a position then to meet these sorts of difficulties, however great they may appear (and indeed they are no less pressing in respect of all the others who have ever treated this matter,† provided that we consider well that all contingent propositions have reasons *for being so rather than otherwise, or (which is the same thing) that they have proofs *a priori* of their truth which make them certain, and† which show that the connection of the subject and the predicate of these propositions has its foundation in the nature of the one and the other; but that they do not have demonstrations of necessity, since these reasons are only founded *on the principle of contingency or of the existence of things, that is to say† on what is or appears the best among several equally possible things; whereas necessary truths are founded on the principle of contradiction and on the possibility or impossibility[a] of essences themselves, without regard in this to the free Will of God or of creatures.

XIV. God produces different substances according to the different views which he has of the universe, and by the intervention of God the nature proper to each substance carries with it that what happens to one corresponds to what happens to all the others, without their acting immediately on one another.

Having come to know in some fashion in what the nature of substances consists, we must next try to explain the dependence which they have on one another, and their actions and passions. Now in the first place it is very obvious that created substances depend on God who conserves them and also produces them continually by a kind of emanation, as we produce our thoughts. For God turn-

[a] [Provided, I say, that one considers these distinctions of things in themselves] without regard . . .

ing so to say on all sides and in every fashion the general system of phenomena which he finds it good to produce *to manifest his glory†, and looking at all the faces of the world in all possible ways since there is no bearing on it which escapes his omniscience, the result of each view of the universe, as looked at from a certain place, is a substance which expresses the universe conformably with this view, if God finds it good to make his thought effective and to produce this substance. And as God's view is always true, our perceptions are true also, but it is our judgements which are of ourselves and which deceive us.

*Now we have said above and it follows from what we have just said, that† each substance is like a world apart, independent of any other thing save God; thus all our phenomena, that is to say all that can ever happen to us, are only consequences of *a*our being. These phenomena maintain a certain order *in conformity with our nature, or so to say with the world which is in us,† and this enables us *to make observations which are useful for regulating our conduct and are justified by the success of future phenomena, and thus often† to judge the future by the past without making mistakes. This would therefore suffice for saying that these phenomena are true, without troubling ourselves about *whether they are outside us and† whether others perceive them also. Yet it is very true that the perceptions or *b*expressions of all substances mutually correspond, so that each *carefully† following certain reasons or laws which it has observed agrees with the other *doing the same, as when several people, having agreed to meet at a certain place on a certain prearranged day, are able to do so effectively if they wish. Now although all express the same phenomena,† their expressions do not *therefor† have to be perfectly alike, but *it is enough that† they should be proportional; as several spectators believe that they are seeing the same thing, *and in fact

a [our nature, and since we are free substances, of our will]
b [qualities]

understand each other,† although each sees *and speaks† according to the measure of his view.

Now there is none but God (from whom *a*all individuals emanate continually *and who sees the universe not only as they see it but also quite differently from all of them†) to be the cause of this correspondence of their phenomena, and to make what is private to one public to all; *otherwise there would be no communication [1].† It could therefore be said *in some sort, and in a good sense, although remote from ordinary usage,† that a particular substance never acts on another particular substance, nor is acted on by it, if we consider that what happens to each one is only a consequence of its *b*idea *or complete notion† alone, since this idea *already includes all predicates or events and† expresses the whole universe. In fact nothing can happen to us but *thoughts and† perceptions, and all our *future thoughts and† perceptions are only consequences, *albeit contingent,† of our preceding thoughts and perceptions, such that if I were capable of considering distinctly everything that is happening *or appearing† to me at this moment, I should be able to see therein everything that will happen or appear to me for ever after; *nor would it fail but would happen to me in the very same way, though everything outside me were destroyed, provided that there remained only God and myself.† But since we attribute to other things, *as to causes acting on us,† what we perceive in a certain manner, we must consider the ground of this judgement and how much truth there is in it.*c*

a [all substances]   *b* [nature/essence/idea] alone . . .
c *Long passage suppressed by Leibniz before the copies were taken:*

It is a fact especially that when we desire some *c'*phenomenon and it happens at the right time, and this takes place ordinarily, we say that we have acted and been the cause of it, as when I will*c"* what is called moving my hand. Also when it seems to me that *by my

---

[1] "liaison".

DISCOURSE ON METAPHYSICS

will† something happens to what I call another substance, *and that this would have happened to it thereby, as I judge by frequent experience,† even if it had not wanted it, I say that this substance is passive, as I admit of myself when this happens to me according to the will of another substance. Also when we have willed something that happens and there also follows some other thing which we did not will, we still say that we did this, provided that we understand how it followed from the first. There are also some phenomena of extension which we attribute to ourselves more particularly and of which the ground *a parte rei* is called our body, and as everything of note that happens to it, that is to say all the notable changes which appear to us in it, are felt strongly, at least ordinarily, we attribute to ourselves all the passions of this body, and that with good reason, for even if we did not perceive them at first, we do not fail to perceive well the consequences, as when we have been transported from one place to another asleep. We also attribute to ourselves the actions of this body, as when we run, strike, fall, and *e‴*our body, continuing the motion that has been begun, makes some effect. But I do not attribute to myself what happens to other bodies since I perceive that large changes can happen which are not sensible to me, unless my body is exposed to them in a certain way which I conceive to be appropriate to them.

Thus it is clear that although all the bodies in the universe belong to us in some fashion and sympathise with our body, we do not attribute to ourselves what happens to them. For when my body is pushed, I say I have myself been pushed, but if some other body is pushed, although I perceive it and this produces some passion in me, I do not say I have been pushed, for I measure the place where I am by that of my body. And this language is very reasonable, for it is appropriate for expressing oneself plainly in ordinary practice. It can be said in a few words as to the spirit that our wills and judgements *or reasonings† are actions, but our perceptions or sentiments are passions; and as to the body we say that change that happens to it is an action when it is the consequence of a preceding change, but otherwise it is a passion.

In general, to give our terms a sense which reconciles metaphysics to practice, when several powers are affected by the same change (as indeed every change concerns them all), one can say that the power which passes thereby to a greater degree of perfection or continues in the same degree is active, but that which becomes thereby immediately more limited, so that its expressions become more confused, is passive.

e′ [perception]
e″ [that there should appear to me]
e‴ [this impetus]

26 DISCOURSE ON METAPHYSICS

XV. ^a*The action of one ^bfinite substance on another consists only in the increase in the degree of its expression conjoined with the diminution of that of the other, in as much as God ^chas so formed them in advance that they accommodate themselves to one another.*

But without embarking on a long discussion it is enough for the present, in order to reconcile metaphysical language with practice, to remark that we attribute more to ourselves, ^d*and with reason, the phenomena which we express more perfectly, and that we attribute to other substances that which each expresses best. Thus a substance which is of infinite extent in as much as it expresses everything, becomes limited by the more perfect or less perfect manner of its expression. It is thus that one can conceive that substances hinder or limit one another, and consequently one can say that in this sense they act on one another and are compelled **so to speak†† to accommodate themselves to one another. For it can happen that a change which augments the expression of the one diminishes that of the other. Now the virtue of a particular substance is to express well the glory of God, and it is by this that it is less limited. ^eAnd each thing, when it exerts its virtue or power, that is to say when it acts, changes for the better and extends itself in as much as it acts :† thus when a change happens by which several substances are affected (as indeed every change concerns them all), I believe one can say that the substance which passes immediately thereby to a greater degree of perfection *or to a more perfect expression exerts its power and† *acts*, and that which

^a [Substances being limited, in as much as they express God and the universe imperfectly, hinder one another and are obliged to accommodate themselves to one another.]

^b [created]   ^c [compels them to] accommodate

^d [the clearer and more distinct perceptions, and likewise one can in general attribute more to a substance the clearer and more distinct expressions]

^e [Now all action consists in a variation,] and each thing when it exercises its virtue or power [without being hindered or limited,] that is to say . . .

passes to a lesser degree *makes known its weakness and†
is passive. I also hold that every action *of a substance
which has perception† involves some *pleasure*, and every
passion some *pain*, and *vice versa*, yet it can well happen
that a present advantage is destroyed by a greater
evil in the sequel. *Whence it comes that one can sin
in acting **or exerting one's power,†† and in finding
pleasure.†

*XVI. The extraordinary concourse of God is comprised in what
our essence expresses, for this expression extends to everything, but
it surpasses the forces of our nature or our distinct expression, which
is finite and follows certain subordinate maxims.*

There only remains at present to explain ^ahow *it is
possible that† God should sometimes have influence on
men *or on other substances† by an extraordinary and
miraculous concourse, *since it seems that nothing extraordinary or supernatural can happen to them, seeing that
all their events are only consequences of their nature.†
But we must remember what we said above with regard
to miracles in the universe, which are always in conformity
with the universal law and the general order, although
they are above subordinate maxims. And in as much as
every person *or substance† is like a little world which
expresses the great world, one can say likewise that this
^bextraordinary action *of God on this substance† is
none the less miraculous, although it is comprised in the
general order of the universe in as much as it is expressed^c
by *the essence or† individual notion of this substance.
*That is why if we comprise in our nature all that it expresses, nothing is supernatural to it, for it extends to

^a [how God has influence on man by his grace, since it appears
that all that is to happen to him must be natural to him in as much
as it is a consequence of his substance.]
^b [extraordinary concourse is] comprised in the general order . . .
^c [by the nature of this person]

everything : **an effect always expressing its cause, and God being the true cause of substances.†† But as what our nature expresses more perfectly belongs to it in a peculiar manner, since it is therein that its power consists **and that it is limited,†† as I have just explained, there are many things which surpass the forces of our nature and even those of all limited natures. Consequently in order to speak more clearly† I say that miracles and the extraordinary concourses of God have this peculiarity that they cannot be foreseen*a* by the reasoning of any created spirit, however enlightened it might be, because distinct comprehension of the general order surpasses all of them : whereas everything that is called natural depends on less general maxims that creatures can understand. *b*In order that the words may be as irreproachable as the sense, it would be well to link certain ways of speaking with certain thoughts, and that which comprises all that we express might be called our essence or idea, and as it expresses our union with God himself, it has no limits and nothing surpasses it. But what is limited in us could be called our nature or our power, and in this regard what surpasses the natures of all created substances is supernatural.

*XVII. Example of a subordinate maxim or law of nature. In which it is shown that God always conserves *regularly† the same force but not the same quantity of motion, against the Cartesians and several others.*

I have already made frequent mention of subordinate maxims, or laws of nature, and it seems that it would be well to give an example of them : our new philosophers commonly use the famous rule*c* that God always conserves

a [and deduced]
b [In order to say nothing about these maxims or about the laws of nature which might offend,]
c [advanced by Mons. Des Cartes]

the same quantity of motion in the world.¹ Indeed it is very plausible, and in the past I held it to be indubitable. But I have since recognised in what the mistake consists. It is that Monsieur des Cartes and many other able mathematicians believed that quantity of motion^a, that is to say speed multiplied by size of the moving body, agrees entirely with motive force, *or to speak geometrically that forces are in a compound ratio of speeds and bodies.† Now it is very ^{b}reasonable that the same force should always be conserved in the universe^c. Also, if we attend to phenomena ², we see that there is no perpetual mechanical motion because, if there were, the force of a machine, *which is always being diminished a little by friction and must soon finish, would make itself good and consequently† would increase of itself without any new impulse from outside; and we also notice that the force of a body is only diminished in the measure that it gives it to contiguous bodies *or to its own parts in so far as they have separate motion.†

Thus they believed that what can be said of force could also be said of quantity of motion. But, to show the difference between them, I suppose that a body falling from a certain height acquires the force to rise to it again, if its direction so carries it, *unless there are any hindrances†; for example a pendulum would rise again *perfectly† to the height from which it descended, if the resistance of the air and some other small obstacles did not diminish by a little its acquired force.

I suppose also that as much force is required to lift a

^{a} [was the same thing as force, or at least, expressed it perfectly]
^{b} [obvious]
^{c} [since taking the whole universe nothing resists it]

---

¹ *In this article, as elsewhere, Leibniz's wording has been strictly reproduced (that is to say, the technical terms of present-day dynamics have not been substituted), but a brief exposition of the argument has been given in the Introduction, p. xxiii, in which the appropriate modern terms have been indicated.*
² *i.e. in modern terms, if we turn from a priori to empirical considerations.*

body A of one pound to the height CD of four fathoms, as to raise a body B of four pounds to the height EF of one fathom. All this is granted by our new philosophers.

It is thus obvious that the body A having fallen from the height CD has acquired precisely as much force as the body B fallen from the height EF; *for the body (B) having reached F and having the force to rise again to E (by the first supposition), has consequently the force to carry a body of four pounds, that is to say its own body, to the height EF of one fathom, and likewise the body (A) having reached D and having the force to rise again to C, has the force to carry a body of one pound, that is to say its own body, to the height CD of four fathoms. Therefore (by the second supposition) the force of the two bodies is equal.†

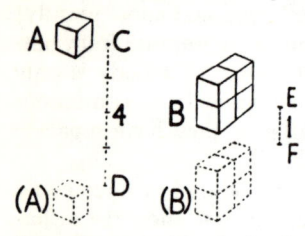

Let us see now whether the quantity of motion is also the same on both sides: but here we shall be surprised to find a very great difference. For it was demonstrated by Galileo that the speed acquired by the fall CD is double the speed acquired by the fall EF, although the height is quadruple. Let us then multiply the body A which is as 1 by its speed which is as 2, the product or the quantity of motion will be as 2, and on the other side multiply the body B which is as 4 by its speed which is as 1, the product or quantity of motion will be as 4; thus the quantity of motion of the body (A) at the point D is half the quantity of motion of the body (B) at the point F, and yet their forces are equal; *thus there is a great difference between quantity of motion and force;† which had to be shown.

*We can see by this how force must be measured by the quantity of the effect which it can produce, for example by the height to which a heavy body of a certain size and kind can be lifted, which is very different from the speed which it can be given. And to give it double the speed requires more than double the force.†

Nothing is simpler than this proof; and *a*Mons. des Cartes only fell into error here *b*because he trusted his thoughts too much when they were not yet mature enough. But I am surprised that his disciples have not perceived this mistake since : and I am afraid that they are gradually beginning to imitate *some of† the Peripatetics *whom they scoff at† and are growing like them into the habit of consulting the books of their master rather than reason and nature.

XVIII. The distinction between force and quantity of motion is important inter alia *for judging that we must have recourse to metaphysical considerations separate from extension in order to explain the phenomena of bodies.*

This consideration of force distinguished from quantity of motion is very important, not only *in natural philosophy and mechanics† for finding true laws of nature and rules of motion *and even for correcting several errors of practice which have crept into the writings of some able mathematicians,† but also in metaphysics for understanding the principles better. For motion, *if one considers in it only what it comprises precisely and formally, that is to say a change of place,† is not an entirely real thing, and when several bodies change situation among themselves, it is not possible to determine by consideration of these changes alone to which among them motion and rest must be attributed, *as I could show geometrically if I wished to stay for it now.†

But force or the proximate cause of these changes is some-

a [it is doubtless by precipitation that]
b [by his accustomed confidence, founded on the happy success of some of his meditations/thoughts, and on the experience he had of the penetration of his spirit which in the end made him a little too bold]

thing more real, and there is enough ground for attributing it to one body rather than to another ; hence it is only by this that one can know to which the motion belongs more. Now this force is something different from size, figure and motion, and one can judge thereby that all that is conceived in a body does not consist uniquely in extension and its modifications, as our moderns are persuaded. Thus we are further obliged to re-establish certain beings or forms which they have banished. And it becomes more and more apparent, although all particular phenomena of nature can be explained mathematically or mechanically by those who understand them, that nevertheless the general principles of corporeal nature and of mechanics itself are rather metaphysical than geometrical, and belong rather to some indivisible forms or natures as causes of appearances than to corporeal or extended mass. A reflection which is capable of reconciling the mechanical philosophy of the moderns with the circumspection of some intelligent and well-intentioned persons who fear with some reason that we are getting too far away from immaterial beings, to the prejudice of piety.

XIX. *Utility of final causes in Natural Philosophy.*

As I do not like to judge people in bad part, I do not accuse our new philosophers[a], who claim to banish final causes from natural philosophy, but I am nevertheless obliged to own [b]*that the consequences of this sentiment seem to me dangerous, especially when I connect it with the one that I have refuted at the beginning of this discourse which seems to tend to remove final causes altogether, as if God intended no end or good in acting or as if the good were not the object of his will.† And for myself I hold on the contrary that it is there that the principles

[a] [of impiety]
[b] [that I do not recognise in it their spirit and their ordinary prudence, I am willing to own that it is not for man alone that everything is done]

of all existences and of the laws of nature must be sought, because God always intends the best and the most perfect.

I am willing to admit that we are prone to deceive ourselves when we try to determine the ends or counsels of God, but that is only when we try to limit them to some particular design, believing that he only had a single thing in view, whereas he has regard for everything at the same time ; *as when we believe that God made the world for us alone, **this is a great mistake,†† though it is very true that he made it **in all its entirety†† for us and that there is nothing in the universe which does not concern us and does not accommodate itself also to the regard which he has for us, according to the principles set out above.† Thus when we see some good effect or some perfection which happens, or which follows from the works of God, we can surely say that God intended it. For he *does nothing by chance and† is not like us, who sometimes slip and fail to do good. That is why, far from making a mistake in this, *as do the extreme politicians who imagine too much refinement in the designs of Princes, or the commentators who seek too much erudition in their author, we cannot attribute too much reflection to this infinite wisdom, and† there is no matter in which there is less error to fear while we only make affirmations, and provided that in it we avoid negative propositions which limit the designs of God.

All who see the admirable structure of animals find themselves drawn to recognise the wisdom of the author of things, and I advise those who have some sentiment of piety *and even of true Philosophy,† to keep away from the language of some would-be free-thinkers [1] who say that we see because we happen to have eyes, without the eyes having been made to see. When one is seriously given to these sentiments which ascribe everything to the necessity of matter or to a certain chance (although both must

[1] " esprits forts "

appear ridiculous to those who understand what we have explained above), it is difficult to be able to recognise an intelligent author of nature. *For the effect must correspond to its cause, and it is even best known by knowledge of its cause,† and it is unreasonable to introduce a sovereign intelligence ordering all things and then, instead of using his wisdom, only to use the properties of matter to explain phenomena. As if, to account for the victory of a great Prince in taking some important stronghold, an historian were to say that it was because the corpuscles of gunpowder, being released at the touch of a spark, escaped with a speed capable of throwing a hard heavy body against the walls of the stronghold, while the branches of the corpuscles which make up the copper of the cannon were so well interlaced as not to tear asunder by this speed; instead of showing how the foresight of the victor made him choose the suitable time and means, and how his power surmounted all obstacles.

XX. Memorable passage of Socrates in the Phaedo of Plato against over-materialist philosophers.

This reminds me of a fine passage of Socrates in the Phaedo of Plato, which conforms marvellously with my sentiments on this point, and seems to be written expressly against our over-materialist Philosophers. Its relevance here has made me want to translate it, though it is rather long, so that perhaps this specimen will give occasion to someone to acquaint us with the many other fine and sound thoughts in the writings of this famous author.[1]

[1] *In the copy there is a blank space at this point, according to Gerhardt, and § 21 follows. Lestienne reports that in the autograph MS. there is the marginal note:* " Inseratur locus ex Phaedone Platonis ubi Socrates Anaxagoram irridet, qui mentem introducit nec ea utitur." *Lestienne draws attention to a résumé in French and Latin of the Phaedo made by Leibniz in March 1676 (Foucher de Careil:* " *Nouvelles lettres et opuscules* ", *p. 45*), *and to the translation of a passage of the Phaedo into French printed by Gerhardt (VII, 335, part of Fragment XVI). He concludes that this latter was the*

"I heard someone reading one day, he said, from a book of Anaxagoras, where there were these words, *that an intelligent being was the cause of all things, and that he had disposed and adorned them*. This pleased me exceedingly, for I thought that if the world was the effect of an intelligence, everything would be done in the most perfect manner that was possible. That is why I believed that whoever wished to explain why things beget one another or perish or subsist, would have to look for what was suitable to the perfection of each thing. Thus a man would only have to consider in himself or in any thing else what would be the best and the most perfect. For he who knew the most perfect would thereby easily judge what was imperfect, because there is only one and the same knowledge of the one and the other.

"Considering all this, I rejoiced at having found a master who could teach me the reasons of things: for example whether the earth is round rather than flat, and why it was better that it should be so rather than otherwise. I expected further that in saying whether the earth is at the centre of the universe or not, he would explain to me why that was the most suitable. And that he would tell me as much of the sun, the moon, the stars and their motions. And that finally, having shown me what was suitable to each thing in particular, he would show me what would be best in general.

"Full of this hope I took and I read through the works of Anaxagoras very eagerly, but I found myself a long way out in my reckoning, for I was surprised to see that he made no use of this governing intelligence which he had put forward, that he said no more of the adornment or of the perfection of things, and that he introduced certain ethereal matters that had little plausibility.

"In which he did as the man who having said that

passage intended by Leibniz for insertion here, and reproduces it following Gerhardt. We re-translate from Leibniz's translation. The passage is Phaedo 97b–99c. There are a few omissions.

Socrates does things intelligently, and afterwards going on to explain in particular the causes of his actions, would say that he is seated here because he has a body composed of bones, skin and sinews, that the bones are solid but they have gaps or joints, that the sinews can be tightened and relaxed, and that is why the body is flexible and finally why I am sitting here. Or if, wishing to account for this present discourse, he were to have recourse to the air, the organs of speech and hearing, and similar things, forgetting meanwhile the true causes, namely that the Athenians have believed that they would do better to condemn me rather than to acquit me, and that I myself have believed that I did better to stay sitting here than to flee. For by my faith, but for this, these sinews and bones would have been with the Boeotians and Megarians long since, if I had not found that it is more just and nobler on my part to suffer the penalty which my country wishes to impose on me than to live elsewhere vagabond and exiled. That is why it is unreasonable to call these bones and sinews and their movements causes.

"It is true that he who should say that I could not do all this without bones and sinews would be right, but the true cause is something else, and this is only a condition without which the cause could not be a cause.

"People who only say, for example, that the whirling motion of bodies keeps the earth where it is, forget that the divine power disposes everything in the finest way, and do not understand that it is the good and the beautiful which joins, which forms, and which maintains the world." Thus far Socrates, for what follows in Plato of ideas or forms is not less excellent, but is a little more difficult.

XXI. If mechanical rules depended on Geometry alone without Metaphysics, phenomena would be quite different.

Now since the wisdom of God has always been recognised in the detail of the *mechanical† structure of some particular bodies, it ought also to show itself in the general economy of the world and in the constitution of the laws of nature. This is so true that one notices the counsels of this wisdom in the laws of motion in general. For if there were nothing in bodies but extended mass, and if there were nothing in motion but change of place, and if everything had to be and could be deduced from these definitions *alone by a geometric necessity†, it would follow, as I have shown elsewhere,[1] that the smaller body would give to the greater which was at rest and which it met, the same speed that it had, without losing anything of its own speed; and a number of other such rules would have to be admitted quite contrary to the formation of a system. But the decree of divine wisdom to conserve always the same force and the same direction *in sum†[2] has provided for this.

I even find that several effects of nature can be demonstrated doubly, namely by consideration of the efficient cause, and also separately by consideration of the final cause, using *for example† the decree of God always to produce his effect in the easiest *and most determined† ways, as I have shown elsewhere[3] in accounting for the rules of catoptrics and dioptrics,[4] and of which I shall say more soon.

XXII. *Reconciliation of the two ways, *of which the one goes† by final causes and *the other† by efficient causes, in order to [a]satisfy both those who explain nature mechanically and those who have recourse to incorporeal natures.*

It is well to make this remark, to reconcile those who hope to explain mechanically the formation of the [b]first

[a] [defend]　　　　　　　　　　[b] [foetus]

---

[1] *in his "Theoria motus abstracti", which is the second section of the work "Hypothesis physica nova . . ." Mainz 1671 (Gerhardt, IV, 221).*

[2] *for an explanation of this term see Introduction, p. xxv.*

[3] *in " Unicum opticae, catoptricae et dioptricae principium ", a short essay published in the Leipzig journal " Acta Eruditorum " in 1682. (The collected works edited Dutens, III, 145.)*　　　　[4] *i.e. of reflection and refraction.*

tissue of an animal and of the whole machine of the parts, with those who explain this same structure by final causes. Both are good, both can be useful, not only for admiring the work of the great artificer, but also for discovering useful things in natural philosophy and in Medicine. And the authors who follow these different paths ought not to malign each other.

For I see that those who apply themselves to explaining the beauty of the divine Anatomy mock at others who imagine that a movement of certain fluids *that seems fortuitous† could make so fair a variety of limbs, and call these people rash and profane. And the latter on the contrary call the former simple and superstitious, as were those ancients who took men of science [1] to be impious, when they maintained that it is not Jupiter that thunders, but some matter present in the clouds. The best would be to connect the one and the other consideration, for if it is permissible to use a mean comparison, I recognise and I exalt the skill of a workman not only in showing what designs he had in making the parts of his machine, but also in explaining the instruments he used to make each part, especially when these instruments are simple and ingeniously contrived. *And God is an able enough artisan* to produce a machine a thousand times more ingenious than that of our body, while only using some quite simple fluids formed expressly in such a way that only the ordinary laws of nature are required to arrange them in the right way to produce so admirable an effect, but it is also true that this would not happen at all [a] if God were not the author of nature.

Yet I find that the way of efficient causes, *which is indeed deeper and in some fashion more immediate and *a priori*, pays the price of being† difficult enough in matters of detail, and I believe that our Philosophers are still

[a] [or seldom] *added, then deleted*

[1] " physiciens ".

for the most part far away from it. But the way of final causes is easier, and is not infrequently of use for discerning important *and useful† truths which one would be a long time in finding by the other *more physical [1]† route, of which Anatomy can furnish some notable examples. Thus I hold that Snellius [2] who was the first discoverer of the rules of refraction[a] would have waited a long time to find them if he had first tried to find how light is formed. But he apparently followed the method which the ancients used for catoptrics, which is in fact by final causes. For seeking the easiest way to conduct a ray from a given point to another given point by reflection from a given plane, *(supposing that to be the design of nature)†, they found the equality of the angles of incidence and of reflection, *as may be seen in a little treatise of Heliodorus of Larissa [3] and elsewhere.† Mons. Snellius as I believe, and after him (although without knowing anything about him) M. Fermat,[4] applied this more ingeniously to refraction. For when the rays observe *in the same media† the same proportion of the sines, *which is also that of the resistances of the media,† this is found to be the easiest way, *or at least the most determined,† for passing from a given point in one medium to a given point in another.

[a] [which he had taught publicly in Holland (although death prevented him from publishing the work which is known to have been finished)] *added, then deleted*

---

[1] " physique " (*adj*) ; *the noun is elsewhere translated* " natural philosophy ".

[2] *W. Snell van Royen (1591–1626), Dutch mathematician celebrated for his discovery about 1620 of the laws of refraction, which he communicated in lectures at the University of Leyden.*

[3] " *Damiani philosophi Heliodori larissaei de Opticis libri duo* ", *ed. Bartholin, Paris, 1657. Heliodorus and (his son or pupil?) Damianos, Greek mathematicians probably of 4th century A.D. The edition of 1657 includes a fragment on reflection apparently from the Catoptrics of Hero of Alexandria, and a modern abridgement of Euclid, taken from a forged manuscript (Pauly-Wissowa, IV, 2).*

[4] *Pierre de Fermat (1601–65). His main works were published posthumously by his son in 1670 and 1679.*

And the demonstration of this same theorem that M. des Cartes tried to give *by the way of efficient causes† is far from being as good. At least there is room for suspicion that he would never have found it in this way if he had learnt nothing in Holland of the discovery of Snellius.

XXIII. To return to immaterial substances, it is explained how God acts on the understanding of spirits, and whether we always have the idea of what we think.

I have found it apposite to insist a little on these considerations of final causes, *incorporeal natures, and *a* an intelligent cause, with reference to bodies,† to make known their use even in natural philosophy and mathematics, in order for the one part to purge mechanical philosophy from the profanity imputed to it, and for the other part to elevate the spirits of our philosophers from material considerations alone to nobler meditations. It will be apposite now to return from bodies to immaterial natures and particularly to spirits, and to say something of the means which God uses to enlighten them and act on them, in which it must not be doubted but that there are also certain laws of nature, of which I could speak more fully elsewhere. It will suffice now to touch somewhat on ideas—whether we see everything in God, and how God is our light.

Now it will be apposite to remark that the misuse of ideas occasions several errors. For when we reason about something we imagine that we have an idea of this thing, and that is the foundation on which some Philosophers *both ancient and modern† have built a certain demonstration of God which*b* is very imperfect. For they say, it must be that I have an idea of God or of a perfect being since I think of him and one cannot think without an idea ; *now the idea of this being contains all perfections, and existence is one, consequently he exists.† But as we often think of impossible chimeras, for example the highest

a [intelligent causes] *b* [to speak rigorously]

degree of speed, the greatest number, the meeting of the conchoid with its base or axis, this reasoning is insufficient. It is then in this sense that one can say that there are true and false ideas, according as the thing in question is possible or not. And it is when we are assured of its possibility that we can boast of having an idea of the thing. Thus the above argument proves at least that God exists necessarily if he is possible. Which is indeed an excellent privilege of the divine nature, only to need its possibility or essence in order to exist actually, *and this is precisely what is called *Ens a se*.†

XXIV. What is knowledge clear or obscure, distinct or confused, adequate or inadequate, intuitive or suppositive; and definition nominal, real, causal, essential.

In order the better to understand the nature of ideas, we must touch somewhat on the varieties of knowledge. ᵃWhen I can recognise a thing among others, without being able to say in what its differentiae or properties consist, the knowledge is *confused*. It is thus that we sometimes know **clearly*, without being in any way in doubt,† whether a poem or a picture is good or bad, because there is a *je ne sais quoi* which satisfies us or offends us. But when I can explain the marks which I have, the knowledge is called *distinct*. And such is the knowledge of an assayer, who discerns true gold from false by means of certain tests or marks which make up the ᵇdefinition of gold.

But distinct knowledge has degrees, for ordinarily the notions which enter into the definition are themselves in need of definition, and are only known confusedly. But when everything that enters into a definition or into dis-

---
ᵃ [When I only know the possibility of a thing by experience, the idea/knowledge which I have of it is confused, because all that exists is possible. It is thus that we know bodies and their qualities. But when I can prove the possibility *a priori*, this knowledge is distinct.]
ᵇ [nominal]

tinct knowledge is known distinctly, down to the primary notions, I call this knowledge *adequate*. And when my spirit comprehends at the same time *and distinctly *all the primary ingredients† of a notion, it has *intuitive* knowledge of it, which is very rare, the greater part of human knowledge only being *confused or† *suppositive*.

It is also well to distinguish nominal and real definitions : I call that a *nominal definition* when one can still doubt whether the defined notion is possible, as for instance when I say that an endless screw is a solid line,^b the parts of which are congruent *or can be superimposed on one another ;† the man who does not know from elsewhere what an endless screw is, could doubt whether such a line is possible, although in fact it is a reciprocal property of the endless screw, *for the other lines of which the parts are congruent (which are only the circumference of the circle and the straight line) are plane, that is to say can be described *in plano*.† This shows that any reciprocal property can serve as a nominal definition, but when the property makes known the possibility of the thing, it makes the definition real ; *and while one only has a nominal definition one cannot be sure of the consequences that are drawn from it, for if it concealed some contradiction or impossibility, opposite conclusions could be drawn from it. That is why truths do not depend on names and are not arbitrary as some of our modern philosophers [1] have believed.†

Furthermore there is still a great difference between *species of† real definitions, for when the possibility is only

---

^a all [this analysis] of a notion . . .
Marginal note by Leibniz in the autograph MS.: N.B. Notio media inter intuitivam et claram est cum omnium notionum impedientium falli claram cognitionem habeo.[2]

^b [that is to say which passes through several parallel planes]

---

[1] e.g. *Hobbes*.
[2] "A notion is intermediate between intuitive and clear when I have clear knowledge of all the notions which prevent me from being deceived."

proved by experience as in the definition of *a**quicksilver, of which we know the possibility because we know that such a body is in fact found **which is an extremely heavy but nevertheless rather volatile fluid††, † the definition is merely real and nothing more; but when the possibility is proved *a priori*, the definition is real and also causal,*b* *as when it contains the possible generation of the thing.† And when it takes the analysis to its end, down to primary notions, without supposing anything which has need of proof *a priori*† of its possibility, the definition is perfect or *essential*.

XXV. In what case our knowledge is joined with contemplation of the idea.

Now it is obvious that we have no idea of a notion which is impossible. And when the knowledge is only *suppositive*, even if we do have the idea, we do not contemplate it, for such a notion is only known in the same way as *occultly† impossible [1] notions, *and if it is possible, it is not through this manner of knowing that we learn of its possibility.† For example if I think of a thousand, or of a chiliagon, I *often† do so without contemplating the idea of it (as when I say that a thousand is ten times a hundred), without giving myself the trouble of thinking*c* what 10 and 100 are, because *I suppose* it to be known and do not believe that at present I need stay to conceive them. Thus it could well happen, as indeed it does happen *often enough,† that I deceive myself with regard to a notion which I suppose or believe I understand, whereas in truth it is impossible *or at least incompatible with the others with which I connect it,† and whether I

---

a [gold, it is still rather imperfect,] but when the possibility . . .
b [or essential]
c [of the definition of] 10 . . .

---

[1] *i.e. notions containing a concealed impossibility.*

deceive myself or not this suppositive manner of conceiving remains the same. It is only then when our knowledge is *clear* in confused notions or when it is *intuitive* in distinct notions that we see the whole idea of it.[a]

XXVI. *That we have in us all ideas; and of Plato's reminiscence.*

In order to conceive well what an idea is, we must forestall an equivocation, for some take the idea for the form or differentia of our thoughts, and in this way we have the idea in our spirit only in as much as we think of it, *and every time we think of it anew we have other ideas of the same thing, although similar to the preceding ideas.† But it seems that others take the idea for an immediate object of thought, or for some permanent form which remains when we are not contemplating it. And indeed our soul always has in it the quality of representing to itself any nature or form whatever, when the occasion for thinking of it arises. And I believe that this quality of our soul, in as much as it expresses some nature, form, or essence, is properly the idea of the thing, which is in us and is always in us whether we think of it or no. For our soul expresses God and the universe and all essences as well as all existences.

This agrees with my principles, for nothing ever enters into our spirit naturally from outside, and it is a bad habit that we have, to think as if our soul received certain *messenger† species and as if it had doors and windows. We have all these forms in our spirit all the time, because our spirit always expresses all its future thoughts, *and already thinks confusedly of everything that it will ever think distinctly.† And nothing can be taught us of which we do not have in our spirit the idea, which is as the matter out of which this thought forms itself.

[a] [Yet we have effectively in our spirit all possible ideas and even think of them all the time in a confused manner.]

It is this that Plato excellently well considered, when he put forward his reminiscence, which is very sound provided that it is taken aright and purged of the error of pre-existence *and that we do not imagine that the soul must already have known and thought distinctly at another time what it learns and thinks now.† He also confirmed his sentiment by a fine experiment[1], introducing a little boy[a] whom he leads insensibly to some very difficult truths of Geometry concerning incommensurables without teaching him anything, solely by asking questions in order and appositely. Which shows that our soul *knows all this virtually and† only needs *animadversion* to know truths, and consequently that it has at least the ideas on which these truths depend. It may even be said to possess these truths already, if they are taken as relations of ideas.

XXVII. How our soul can be compared to empty tablets, and how our notions come from the senses.

Aristotle preferred to compare our soul to tablets which are still blank, where there is space for writing[2], *and he maintained that there is nothing in our understanding which does not come from the senses.† That agrees better with popular notions, as is the manner of Aristotle, whereas Plato goes deepér. These sorts of Doxologies [3] *or practicologies† may nevertheless pass in ordinary usage, much as we see that those who follow Copernicus say none the less that the sun rises and sets. I even find that they can often be given a good sense according to which there

[a] [in his dialogue called Meno]

---

[1] *Meno 81e–86b.*

[2] *De Anima, III, 4, 430ᵃ, 1* " *What the mind (nous) thinks must be in it just as the characters may be said to be on a writing-tablet on which as yet nothing stands written*". *To this Leibniz adds in the next phrase the familiar* " *nihil est in intellectu nisi prius fuerit in sensu*". *This does not however occur in any extant text of Aristotle, and must be said to originate from Scholastic tradition.*

[3] *in the sense of "formulae".*

is nothing false in them, as I have already remarked in what way one can say *truly† that *particular† substances act on one another, and in this same sense one can also say that we receive ^aknowledge *from outside† through the agency of the senses, *because some external things contain **or express more particularly†† the reasons which determine our soul to certain thoughts.† But when it is a question of the exactitude of metaphysical truths it is important to recognise the extent *and independence† of our soul, which goes infinitely further ^bthan the vulgar think, although in the ordinary usage of life we only attribute to it what we more obviously perceive and what belongs to us in a particular manner, for there it serves no purpose to go further.

Yet it would be well to choose terms proper to the one and the other sense in order to avoid equivocation. *Thus those^c expressions which are in our soul whether they are conceived or not can be called *ideas*, but those which are conceived or formed can be called *notions, conceptus*.† But in whatever way it is taken it is always false to say that all our notions come from the senses which are called external, for the notion which I have of myself and of my thoughts and consequently of being, substance, action, *identity and many others† come from an internal experience.

XXVIII. God alone is the immediate object of our perceptions which exists outside us, and he alone is our light.

Now in rigorous metaphysical truth there is no external cause which acts on us except God alone^d and he alone

^a [species]

^b [than what we conceive more distinctly, and what we attribute to ourselves more particularly in the ordinary usage of life, where there is no purpose in going further.]

^c [forms]

^d [and one can say that God is the sole immediate external object of our thoughts.]

communicates himself to us immediately by virtue of our continual dependence. From which it follows that there is no other external object which affects our soul *and which immediately excites our perception.† Hence we have in our souls ideas of everything only by virtue of the continual action of God on us, that is to say because every effect expresses its cause and thus the essence of our soul is a certain expression, imitation *or image† of the divine essence, *thought and will,† and of all the ideas which are comprised therein. It can be said then that God alone is our immediate object outside us and that we see all things by him; for example when we see the sun and the stars it is God who has given to us *and conserves for us† the ideas of them and who determines us to think of them effectively *by his ordinary concourse† at the time at which our senses are disposed in a certain manner, according to the laws which he has established. God is the sun and the light of souls, *lumen illuminans omnem hominem venientem in hunc mundum* : [1] and this is not a sentiment new today. After Holy Scripture and the Fathers, who have always been rather for Plato than for Aristotle, I remember *having previously remarked† that in the time of the scholastics, some believed that God is the light of the soul, and according to their way of speaking *intellectus agens animae rationalis*.[2] The Averroists turned it in a bad sense, but others, among whom was I believe William of St. Amour [3] and several mystical Theologians, have taken it in a manner worthy of God and capable of elevating the soul to knowledge of its good.

[1] " The light which lighteth every man that cometh into this world " (*Gospel according to St. John, 1, 9.*)
[2] " the active intelligence of the rational soul."
[3] *Died about 1272, one of the founders of the Sorbonne. Opera, Constance, 1632.*

XXIX. Yet we think *immediately† by our own ideas and not by those of God.

Yet I am not of the sentiment of certain able Philosophers [1] who seem to maintain that our ideas themselves are in God and not in us at all. In my opinion this comes from not having yet considered enough *what we have just explained concerning substances,† nor all the extent *and independence† of our soul, as a result of which it contains everything that happens to it and expresses *[a]* God *and with him all possible and actual beings,† as an effect expresses its cause. Also it is an inconceivable thing that I should think by the ideas of another. The soul must also be affected *effectively† in a certain way when it thinks of something, and it must have in it in advance not only the passive power of being affected in this way, which is already wholly determined, but also an active power in virtue of which it has always had in its nature marks of the future production of this thought and dispositions to produce it in its time. *And all this already includes the idea comprised in this thought.†

XXX. How God inclines our soul without necessitating it; that we have no right to complain, and we must not ask why Judas sins, since this free action is comprised in his notion, but solely why Judas the sinner is admitted to existence in preference to other possible persons. Of the original imperfection *or limitation† before sin, and of the degrees of grace.

As concerns the action of God on the human will there are a number of difficult enough considerations, which it would be tedious to pursue here. Nevertheless here is what can be said in the main. *[b]* God *in concurring in

[a] [the essence of] God
[b] [We must distinguish indifferent, good, and bad actions]

---

[1] e.g. *Malebranche.*

DISCOURSE ON METAPHYSICS

our actions ordinarily† does no more than follow the laws*a* which he has established, that is to say he conserves and produces our*b* being continually, so that thoughts happen to us *spontaneously*c* or freely† in the order which the notion of our individual substance carries with it *in which they could be foreseen from all eternity.† Further, by virtue of the decree which he has made that the will should always tend to the *apparent† good, *expressing or imitating the will of God in certain particular respects† *with regard to which this apparent good always has some truth in it,† he determines our will to the choice *of that which seems the better,† nevertheless without necessitating it. For absolutely speaking, our will, considered as contrasted with necessity, is in a state of indifference, and it has the power to do otherwise or to suspend its action altogether,† the one and the other alternative being *and remaining† possible.

It depends then on the soul to take precautions against the surprises of appearances, by a firm resolve *d*to reflect and not to act or judge in certain encounters except after ripe deliberation. Yet it is true, and it has even been assured from all eternity, that some soul will not make use of this power in such an encounter. But who is to blame? and can it complain of any but itself? For all these complaints after the fact are unjust if they would have been unjust before the fact. Now this soul a little before sinning, would it be seemly for it to complain of God, *e*as if he were determining it to the sin? The determinations of God in these matters being things *f* that cannot be foreseen, whence does it know that it is under a determination to sin, if not when it is already sinning effectively? It is only a matter of not willing, and God could not propose an easier *and juster† condition; *thus all judges, without

---

a [of nature]   *b* [nature]   *c* [and naturally]
d [fortified by the practice of] reflecting . . .
e [who does not determine it to turn away from sin]
f [that are insensible]

seeking the reasons which have disposed a man to have a bad will, only stay to consider by how much this will is bad.† But perhaps it has been assured from all eternity that I shall sin? Answer your question yourself: perhaps not; and without thinking of what you cannot know and can give you no light, act according to your duty which you know.

But another will say, whence comes it that this man will assuredly commit this sin? The reply is easy, it is that otherwise it would not be this man. For God sees from all time that there will be a certain Judas, of whom the notion or idea that God has of him contains [a] this future free action. There only remains then this question, why such a Judas the traitor, who in the idea of God is only possible, exists actually. But to this question no reply is to be expected on earth, except that in general one must say that since God has found it good that he should exist notwithstanding the sin which he foresaw, this evil must recompense itself with interest in the universe, that God will draw from it a greater good, and that it will be found that in sum this sequence of things in which the existence of this sinner is comprised is the most perfect among all the other possible ways. But always to explain[b] the admirable economy of this choice is something that cannot be while we are travellers [c]in this world; it is enough to know it without understanding it. And here is the place to recognise *altitudinem divitiarum*, the depth and the abyss of the divine wisdom[1], without seeking a detail which involves infinite considerations.

Yet it is clear that God is not the cause of evil. For not only after the innocence of men had been lost and original sin had taken possession of the soul but before this, there was a *limitation or† original imperfection con-

[a] [what he will do]   [b] [in detail]
[c] [in this vale of miseries]

---

[1] *Romans, 11, 33. See §31, p. 54, note 1.*

natural to all creatures*a*, *which makes them peccable or capable of error. Thus there is no more difficulty with regard to the supralapsarians [1] than with regard to others. And it is to this, in my opinion, that we must reduce the sentiment of St. Augustin and other authors that the root of evil is in nothingness, that is to say in the privation or limitation of creatures, which God graciously remedies by the degree of perfection which he is pleased to give.†
This grace of God, *whether ordinary or extraordinary,† has its degrees and its measures, it is always efficacious in itself to produce a certain proportionate effect, and further it is always sufficient not only to make us secure from sin, but even to produce salvation, *supposing that man allies himself to it *b*by what is in him ;† but grace is not always sufficient to surmount the *c*inclinations of man, for otherwise he would be as nothing, and this is reserved to absolutely efficient grace alone which is always victorious, *whether it is so by itself or by the congruity of circumstances.†

XXXI.[2] *dOf the motives* [3] *of election, of faith foreseen, of scientia media,*[4] *of the absolute decree, and that all reduces itself*

a to all [particular] creatures [which inclines some to sin and perhaps without the grace of God all spirits would have fallen]
b [by his will]   *c* [will]
d [Of the foresight of merits, of the dispensation of graces]

---

[1] *A sect of Calvinists who held that God's decrees of election and reprobation were not due to the Fall, but preceded it and his prescience of it.*
[2] *This whole section belongs to the second revision.*
[3] *In the sense of the Latin "motiva"—"grounds".*
[4] *"la science moyenne"; a term introduced by the Spanish Jesuit Molina in 1588 for a kind of knowledge intermediate between God's knowledge of actual existents (scientia visionis) and his knowledge of possibles (by simple intelligence), namely his knowledge of what would happen if conditions obtained. This doctrine is the basis of the Molinist solution (adopted with modifications by Suarez) of the problem of efficacious grace and free will; God foresees what attitude man's will would assume if a particular grace were offered to it (Catholic Encyclopedia, VI, 618b and X, 439b).*

*to the reason why God has chosen for *and resolved to admit to†
existence such and such a possible person, the notion of whom
contains such and such a sequence of graces and of free actions,
which puts an end to the difficulties at a single stroke.*

Finally the graces of God are wholly pure graces on which creatures have no claim :[1] however as it is not enough, in order to explain God's choice *which he makes in dispensing these graces†, to have recourse to his *absolute or conditional† foresight of the future actions of men, so also we must not imagine absolute decrees that have no reasonable motive. As concerns foreseen faith or good works, *it is very true that God has only elected those whose faith and charity he foresaw, *quos se fide donaturum praescivit*,[2] but† the same question returns, why God will give to some rather than others the grace of faith or of good works. And as for this [a]knowledge that God has, which is foresight not of faith and good acts but of their matter *and predisposition,† or of what a man would contribute to them from his side *(since it is true that there is diversity on the side of men where there is diversity on the side of grace, and that in fact a man, although he needs to be stimulated to the good and converted, must also act towards it afterwards)†, it seems to some that one could say that God seeing what the man would do without grace or extraordinary assistance, or at least what there will be on his side after discounting grace, might resolve to give grace to those whose natural dispositions were the better or at least the *less imperfect or† less bad. But even if that were the case, one can still say that these natural dispositions, *in as much as they are good,† are the effect of grace,

[a] " science [moyenne] "

---

[1] *The text first continued with what is now part of the penultimate sentence* [Yet] there are certain great reasons . . . *All the rest of the section was interpolated.*

[2] " whom he foreknew he would endow with faith."

although ordinary, God having favoured some more than others; and since he knows well that these natural advantages which he gives will be the motive [1] for grace or extraordinary assistance, according to this doctrine, is it not true that in the end everything is reduced entirely to his mercy?

I believe then *(since we do not know how much or in what way God has regard to natural dispositions in the dispensation of grace)† that the most exact and the surest thing to say, *according to our principles and as I have already remarked†, is that there must be among the possible beings the person of Peter or John, the notion or idea of whom contains all this sequence of ordinary and extraordinary graces and all the rest of these events with their circumstances, and that God was pleased to choose it from among an infinity of other equally possible persons *to exist actually† : after which it seems that there is nothing more to ask and that all difficulties vanish.

For as to this single great question, why God was pleased to choose it among so many other possible persons, one would have to be very unreasonable not to be content with the general reasons which we have given, the detail of which escapes us. Thus instead of having recourse to an absolute decree, which being without reason is unreasonable, or to reasons which do not solve the difficulty completely and need other reasons, the best would be to say in conformity with St. Paul that there are for this certain great reasons of wisdom or congruity which God has observed, and which are *unknown to mortals† and founded on the general order, the aim of which is the greatest perfection of the universe. It is to this that we are taken back by ᵃthe motives of the glory of God and of the manifestation of his justice as well as of his mercy

---

ᵃ [the reasons alleged]

---

[1] *See p. 51, note 3.*

and generally of his perfections, *and finally the immense depth of riches by which St. Paul's soul was ravished [1].†

XXXII. Utility of these principles in the matter of piety and religion.

Furthermore it seems that the thoughts which we have just explained, *and particularly the great principle of the perfection of the operations of God and that of the notion of the substance which contains all its events **with all their circumstances,†† far from harming serve to confirm religion, to dispel very great difficulties, to inflame souls with a divine love† and to elevate spirits to knowledge of incorporeal substances, much more than the hypotheses which have been seen up to now. For we see very clearly that all other substances depend on God, just as thoughts emanate from our substance, that God is all in all, and that he is intimately united with all creatures, *but in the measure of their perfection,† that it is he alone who determines them *from outside† by his influence, and if to act is to determine immediately, one can say in this sense, *in the language of metaphysics,† that God alone operates on me and alone can do good or evil to me, other substances only *a*contributing by reason of these determinations because God, having regard to all, shares his blessings and obliges them to accommodate themselves to one another. Hence God alone brings about liaison and communication of substances, and it is through him that the phenomena of the ones meet and agree with those of the others and consequently that there is reality in our perceptions. But in practice one attributes actions to particular *b*reasons in the

a [being occasional causes]
b [occasional causes]

---

[1] *St. Paul's Epistle to the Romans, 11, 33-34 (A.V.): "O the depth of the riches both of the wisdom and knowledge of God! how unsearchable are his judgements, and his ways past finding out! 34. For who hath known the mind of the Lord? or who hath been his counsellor?"* See also §30.

sense that I have explained above, because it is not necessary always to mention the universal cause in particular cases.

We also see that every substance has a perfect spontaneity *(which becomes liberty in intelligent substances)†, that everything that happens to it is a consequence of its idea or of its being and that nothing determines it except God alone. And that is why a person [1] whose spirit was very elevated and whose holiness is highly revered was in the habit of saying that the soul should often think as if there were nothing but God and itself in the world.

Now nothing gives us a firmer understanding of immortality than this independence *and this extent of the soul,† which shelters it absolutely from all external things, since it alone makes all its world and is sufficient to itself with God; and it is as impossible that it should perish *without annihilation† as it is impossible that the world (of which it is a perpetual living expression) should destroy itself[a]; hence it is impossible that changes in this extended mass which is called our body should do anything to the soul, or that the dissolution of the body should destroy what is indivisible.

[a] [or that an atom should perish]

---

[1] *St. Teresa ; cf. Leibniz to André Morell, 10 Dec. 1696 (G. Grua, " G. W. Leibniz Textes inédits " Paris 1948, p. 103)* : " And as for St. Teresa, you are right to esteem her works. I found in them one day the fine thought that the Soul should conceive things as if there were only God and itself in the world. This yields a reflection which is even notable in philosophy and I employed it usefully in one of my hypotheses."—*Œuvres de Ste. Therese. De la traduction de Monsieur Arnauld d'Andilly, Paris, 1670, 2nd edition, 1676, p. 68 (the passage in question, from Ch. XIII of the Life, reads literally as follows)* : " for at first the soul should take no care but of itself, and nothing can be more useful to it than to consider itself alone in the world with God alone." In the *Complete Works of St. Teresa of Jesus* translated by E. Allison Peers, London, 1946, 1, 77, it reads : " for the utmost we have to do at first is to take care of our soul and to remember that in the entire world there is only God and the soul ".

XXXIII. Explanation of the ^acommerce of the soul and the body, which has passed for inexplicable or for miraculous, and of the origin of confused perceptions.

We also see the unexpected elucidation of the great mystery of the union of the soul and of the body, that is to say how it happens that the passions and actions of the one are accompanied by actions and passions, *or by suitable phenomena,† of the other. For it is impossible to conceive that the one should have influence on the other, and it is not reasonable simply to ^bhave recourse to the extraordinary operation of the universal cause in an ordinary and particular matter. But here is the true reason of it: we have said that everything that happens to the soul and to each substance is a consequence of its notion; hence the idea itself or essence of the soul carries with it that all its appearances or perceptions must be born (*sponte*) from its own nature, and precisely in such a way that they correspond of themselves to what happens in the whole universe, but more particularly* and more perfectly to what happens† in the body which is assigned to it, because, *in some fashion and for a time,† it is according to the relation of other bodies to its own that the soul expresses *the state of† the universe.^c *Which also makes known how our body belongs to us, but without being attached to our essence. And I believe that people who can meditate will judge favourably of our principles for this reason, that they will be able to see easily in what the ^dconnection which there is between the soul and the body consists, which seems inexplicable by any other way.

We also see that the perceptions of our senses, even when they are clear, must necessarily contain some confused sentiment, for as all the bodies in the universe are in sympathy, our own receives the impression of all the others,

---
^a [union] *corrected in the Arnauld correspondence only*
^b [introduce for it an extraordinary concourse of God]
^c [by its essence]
^d [union]

and although our senses are in relation with everything, it is not possible that our soul should be able to attend to everything in particular; that is why our confused sentiments are the result of a variety of perceptions which is altogether infinite. And this is **almost†† like the confused murmur heard by those who approach the seashore, which comes from the assembled repercussions of innumerable waves. Now if of several perceptions (which do not come together to make one) there is none which excels above the others, and if they make impressions which are almost equally strong or equally capable of determining the attention of the soul, it can only perceive them confusedly.†

XXXIV. Of the difference of Spirits from other substances, souls or substantial forms, and that the immortality which is demanded involves memory.

ᵃSupposing that bodies *which make *unum per se*, like man does,† are substances and that they have substantial forms, and that beasts have souls, we are obliged to admit that these souls and these substantial forms cannot perish *entirely†, any more than ᵇ*atoms ᶜor the ultimate parts of matter in the sentiment of other philosophers; for no substance perishes, although it may become quite different.† They also express the whole universe, although more imperfectly than spirits. But the principal difference is that they do not know what they are *nor what they do, and that, being consequently unable to reflect, they cannot discover **necessary and universal†† truths. It is also

---

ᵃ [I do not [yet] undertake to determine whether bodies are substances, *to speak with metaphysical rigour,† or whether they are only *true* phenomena, like the rainbow, nor consequently whether there are substances, souls, or substantial forms, which are not intelligent.] But supposing that . . . (*Deleted by Leibniz from copy B; cf.* § *11*, § *12* and § *35*)

ᵇ [our own soul]

ᶜ [if there are any]

for lack of reflection on themselves ^athat they have no moral quality,† whence it comes that passing through a thousand transformations, almost like a caterpillar which turns into a butterfly, it is all one for morals or practice if they are said to perish, as can also be said physically, when we say that bodies perish by their corruption. But the intelligent soul, knowing what it is and being able to say this *I* which says so much, remains and subsists not merely Metaphysically, *much more than the others,† but it also remains the same morally and makes the same person. For it is the memory or knowledge of this *I* which makes it capable of punishment or reward. Further, the immortality which is demanded *in morals and in religion† does not consist in this perpetual subsistence *alone† which belongs to all substances, for without the memory of what one had been it would not be in any way desirable. Let us suppose that some ^bindividual were to become King of China at one stroke, but on condition of forgetting what he had been, *as if he had just been born anew†, is it not as much in practice, *or as regards the effects which one can perceive,† as if he were to be annihilated and a king of China to be created in his place at the same instant? Which this individual has no reason to desire.

XXXV. Excellence of Spirits, and that God considers them preferably to the other creatures.

But in order to let it be judged by natural reasons that God will always conserve not only our substance ^cbut also our person, that is to say the memory and knowledge of what we are *(although distinct knowledge of it is sometimes suspended in sleep and in fainting)†, morals must be joined to Metaphysics; that is to say God must be

^a [that they do not make a person]
^b [miserable]
^c [as is manifest from the meditations which we have already explained]

considered not only as the principle and cause of all substances *and of all Beings†, but also as chief of all persons *or intelligent substances,† and as the absolute Monarch of the most perfect city or Republic, as is that of the universe *composed of all the spirits together†, God himself being the most accomplished of all Spirits as he is the greatest of all Beings. For assuredly Spirits *a**are the most perfect substances, and those which best express the divinity.† And the whole nature, end, virtue and function of substances being only to express God and the universe, as has been explained enough, there is no room for doubt that substances which express it with knowledge of what they do and are capable of *b*knowing great truths with regard to God and the universe, express it incomparably better than those natures which are either stupid and incapable of knowing truths, or completely destitute of sentiment and of knowledge ; and the difference between intelligent substances and those which are not is as great as that between the mirror and him who sees.

And as God himself is the greatest and wisest of Spirits, it is easy to judge that the Beings with which he can so to speak enter into conversation and even into society, communicating to them his sentiments and his wills in a particular manner and in such a way that they can know and love their benefactor, must concern him infinitely more than all other things which can only pass for instruments of Spirits ; as we see that all *c*wise persons set infinitely more store by a man than by any other thing, however precious it may be, and it seems that the greatest satisfaction that a soul which is otherwise content can have is to see itself loved by others ; *although with regard to God there is this difference, that **his glory and†† our

a [are either the only substances which are present in the world, in which case bodies are only real/true phenomena, or they are at least] the most perfect substances. (*Deleted from copy B ; cf.* § *34*)
b [discovering and]
c [reasonable]

worship can add nothing to his satisfaction, creatures' knowledge of him being only a consequence of his sovereign and perfect felicity, far from **contributing to it or†† being in part the cause.† Yet what is good and reasonable in finite spirits is present eminently in him, and as we should praise a King who preferred to conserve the life of a man rather than of the most precious and rarest of his animals, we must not doubt that the most enlightened and the justest of Monarchs is of the same sentiment.

XXXVI. God is the monarch of the most perfect republic composed of all the Spirits, and the felicity of this city of God is his principal design. *That Spirits express God rather than the world, but that the other substances express the world rather than God.†[1]

Spirits are indeed the most perfectible substances, and their perfections have the peculiarity of hindering one another the least, *or rather that of helping one another, for only the most virtuous could be the most perfect friends† : whence it manifestly follows that God, who always aims at the greatest perfection in general, will have the greatest care for spirits and will give to them, not only in general, but also to each one in particular, the greatest perfection that the universal harmony can permit.

One can also say that God inasmuch as he is a spirit is the origin of existences; otherwise if he lacked the will to choose the best there would be no reason for one possibility to exist in preference to others. Thus the quality that God has of being himself a Spirit, takes precedence of all the other considerations which he can have with regard to creatures; *spirits alone are made in his image and

---

[1] *This sentence is printed in all the editions as part of the heading of the previous section. It is shown by Lestienne as an addition, and as the point in question was also inserted as an addition into this article and is not mentioned in the previous article, we have transferred the sentence under the assumption that Leibniz inadvertently added it to the wrong heading.*

as it were are of his race or like children of the house, since they alone can serve him freely **and act with knowledge in imitation of the divine nature ;†† one spirit alone is worth a whole world since it not merely expresses the world but also knows it and conducts itself in it after the fashion of God. **Such that, although any substance expresses the whole universe, it seems that nevertheless other substances express the world rather than God but that Spirits express God rather than the world.†† And it is because the nature of Spirits is so noble, bringing them as near to the divinity as is possible for mere creatures, that God draws from them infinitely more glory than from all other Beings, or rather the other beings are only the occasion for Spirits to glorify him.

That is why this moral quality of God which makes him the Lord or Monarch of Spirits concerns him so to speak personally in a quite singular manner. It is in this that he becomes human, that he is willing to suffer anthropologies,[1] and that he enters into society with us as a Prince with his subjects ; and this consideration is so dear to him that† the happy and flourishing state of his Empire,[a] which consists in the greatest possible felicity of the inhabitants, becomes the highest of his laws. For felicity is to [b] persons what perfection is to beings. *And if the first principle of the existence of the physical world is the decree to give it the greatest possible perfection, the first [c] design of the moral world or of the City of God which is the noblest part of the universe must be to spread in it the greatest possible felicity.†

It must not then be doubted that God has ordered everything in such a way that Spirits *not only† may live

[a] [is the highest of the subordinate laws of his conduct] which consists . . .
[b] [spirits]
[c] [principle of existence]

---

[1] *See p. 4, note 1.*

always, *which is indispensable, but also that they may conserve their moral quality always,† in order that his city may not lose a single person, as the world does not lose a single substance. And consequently they will always know what they are, otherwise they would not be susceptible of reward or of punishment, which is however the essence of a Republic *and especially of the most perfect where nothing can be neglected.†

Finally God *being at the same time the justest and the most debonair of Monarchs and† only asking a good will, provided that it is sincere *and serious†, his subjects could not wish for a better condition, and to make them perfectly happy he only wants them to love him.

XXXVII. Jesus Christ has disclosed to men the mystery and the admirable laws of the Kingdom of Heaven and the greatness of the supreme felicity which God prepares for those who love him.

The ancient Philosophers had very little knowledge of these important truths; Jesus Christ alone has expressed them divinely well, and in so clear and so familiar a manner that the grossest spirits have conceived them; thus his Gospel has entirely changed the face of human things; he has given us to know the kingdom of heaven or that perfect republic of spirits which merits the title of city of God, the admirable laws of which he has disclosed to us; he alone has shown how much God loves us and with what exactitude he has provided for everything that concerns us; that having care for the sparrows he will not neglect the reasonable creatures who are infinitely more dear to him; that all the hairs of our head are numbered[1]; that heaven and earth will perish rather than the word of God and whatever belongs to the economy of our salva-

---

[1] *Gospel according to St. Matthew, 10, 29–30 (A.V.):* "*Are not two sparrows sold for a farthing? and one of them shall not fall on the ground without your Father. 30. But the very hairs of your head are all numbered.*"

tion be changed¹; that God has more regard for the least of the intelligent souls than for the whole machine of the world; *a*that we must not fear those who can destroy bodies but cannot harm souls, since God alone can make souls happy or unhappy ²; and that in his hands the souls of the just are safe from all the revolutions of the universe, *nothing being able to act on them but God alone†; that none of our actions is forgotten; and that everything is accounted, even to idle words and a spoonful of water well used ³; finally that all must work out for the greatest wellbeing of the good ⁴; that the just will be like suns ⁵ and that neither our senses nor our spirit has ever tasted anything approaching the felicity that God prepares for those who love him.⁶

a [that souls have nothing to fear but God alone]

---

¹ *Mark, 13, 31, and Luke, 21, 33 (A.V.)*: "*Heaven and earth shall pass away, but my words shall not pass away.*"

² *Gospel according to St. Matthew, 10, 28 (A.V.)*: "*And fear not them which kill the body but are not able to kill the soul: but rather fear him which is able to destroy both soul and body in hell.*"

³ *Matthew, 12, 36 (A.V.)*: "*But I say unto you, that every idle word that men shall speak, they shall give account thereof in the day of judgement.*"

Matthew, 10, 42 (A.V.): "*And whosoever shall give to drink unto one of these little ones a cup of cold water only in the name of a disciple, verily I say unto you, he shall in no wise lose his reward.*"

⁴ *St. Paul's Epistle to the Romans, 8, 28 (A.V.)*: "*And we know that all things work together for good to them that love God, to them who are the called according to his purpose.*"

⁵ *Matthew, 13, 43 (A.V.)*: "*Then shall the righteous shine forth as the sun in the kingdom of their Father.*"

⁶ *First Epistle of St. Paul to the Corinthians, 2, 9 (A.V.)*: "*But as it is written, Eye hath not seen, nor ear heard, neither have entered into the heart of man, the things which God hath prepared for them that love him.*"